Discovering Their Voices

Engaging Adolescent Girls
With Young Adult Literature

Marsha M. Sprague
Kara K. Keeling

INTERNATIONAL
Reading Association
800 BARKSDALE ROAD, PO BOX 8139
NEWARK, DE 19714-8139, USA
www.reading.org

The International Reading Association attempts, through its publications, to provide a forum for a wide spectrum of opinions on reading. This policy permits divergent viewpoints without implying the endorsement of the Association.

Executive Editor, Books   Corinne M. Mooney
Developmental Editor   Charlene M. Nichols
Developmental Editor   Tori Mello Bachman
Developmental Editor   Stacey Lynn Sharp
Editorial Production Manager   Shannon T. Fortner
Production Manager   Iona Muscella
Supervisor, Electronic Publishing   Anette Schuetz

Project Editors   Tori Mello Bachman and Cynthia L. Held

Cover   Design, Linda Steere; Photograph, © Digital Vision Photography/Getty Images

Library of Congress Cataloging-in-Publication Data
Sprague, Marsha M.
  Discovering their voices : engaging adolescent girls with young adult literature / Marsha M. Sprague & Kara K. Keeling.
    p. cm.
  Includes bibliographical references and index.
  ISBN 978-0-87207-611-2
  1. Young adult literature--Study and teaching (Secondary)--United States. 2. Teenage girls--Books and reading--United States. 3. Teenage girls--Psychology. 4. Book clubs (Discussion groups) I. Keeling, Kara K. II. Title.
  PN1009.A1S78 2007
  027.62'6--dc22

                                                                        2006103350

CONTENTS

MARSHA M. SPRAGUE received her bachelor's degree in English from Wellesley College, Massachusetts, USA; she holds a master's degree in education from Pennsylvania State University, University Park, Pennsylvania, and a doctorate in educational leadership from the University of Miami, Florida. She has taught in public schools for over 20 years, ranging from kindergarten to high school, and has also served as a staff development trainer and special education consultant for the Department of Defense, Panama Region. Currently she directs the Teacher Preparation Program at Christopher Newport University, Newport News, Virginia, and teaches in the English Department. An author of over 20 articles, her current research focuses on using literature to assist girls' development.

KARA K. KEELING earned her bachelor's degree in English from Carleton College, Northfield, Minnesota; her master's degree in English from Purdue University, West Lafayette, Indiana; and her PhD in English from Indiana University, Bloomington, Indiana. She has taught at Christopher Newport University, Newport News, Virginia, since 1993, specializing in Children's and Young Adult Literature. She is an active member and ongoing presenter at the annual meeting of the Children's Literature Association. She has published articles on books such as Robert Cormier's *The Chocolate War* (1974), among others, and is currently working on two books of her own, one on food in children's literature and one on geography and identity in young adult literature.

L IKE MANY people in the United States, we read Mary Pipher's *Reviving Ophelia: Saving the Selves of Adolescent Girls* after it appeared on the best-seller lists in 1994. Like many other readers of this book, we were appalled at the vivid descriptions of horrific life experiences that were described through the voices of adolescent girls. Still, we rationalized that these were girls receiving counseling and that, therefore, they represented a very small percentage of teenagers. However, as we listened to our children, nieces, children's friends, and students tell us about the world of the adolescent girl in the 1990s, we came to understand that Mary Pipher's girls were actually representative of many young women, including those from privileged, intact families. One of our daughters wrote this poem at age 15:

> the truth about ophelia
>
> ophelia. you beautiful mermaid, the one that got away—
> shining blue on pink skin-petals. dryad, denial, fresh flowers for her
> grave,
> you cold, shivering wet thing,
>   still holding on
>   to love at first sight.
> that was always your way.
>   chilly adolescence,
>   sex on her mind,
> dying each night in the icy deep.
>
> (Dagny Sprague, 1997)

Dagny's poem echoes Pipher's message: Adolescent girls suffer deeply. Many other books published during the 1990s confirmed and expanded our view that girls in the United States are truly in danger. Some of the books' titles reflect the serious problems girls face, such as Sadker and Sadker's *Failing at Fairness: How Our Schools Cheat Girls* (1994), the American Association of University Women (AAUW) reports *How Schools Shortchange Girls* (1995) and *Hostile Hallways: The AAUW Survey on Sexual Harassment in America's Schools* (1993), and

Orenstein's *Schoolgirls: Young Women, Self-Esteem, and the Confidence Gap* (1994).

We began to look for public responses to these grim stories, and we found many of them. In fact, it is clear that the initiatives schools and communities have taken are making changes. The academic achievement gap between girls and boys, particularly in the area of mathematics, is closing. In a few states, girls are actually outperforming boys in achievement tests (Hupp, 2005). Viadero (2006) reports that more girls than boys are now enrolled in colleges across the United States. Yet we know from our own families and from the conversations we have with our high school and college students that girls still face serious problems. In fact, it may be that the increased pressure to conform and do well is taking its toll.

What can be done to help adolescent girls, especially in areas unrelated to academics? As teachers of literature, we have been struck by the reactions of girls when they read about female characters who are suffering. There is an absolute ferocity that accompanies our female high school and college students' recognition of the pressures that girls face. They are able to articulate their reactions, sometimes angrily. This has led us to explore what happens when we consciously introduce adolescents to books that are meant to spark discussion of the issues girls face. In doing this, we have had to consider what the issues are. Using the work of Pipher, Orenstein, Sadker and Sadker, and others, we have identified the central issue: developing an authentic, individual voice even when surrounded by pressures that suppress the voice. These pressures include societal expectations, the role and influence of adults, influence of male and female peers, the pressure to look pretty, and physical and emotional changes that are a crucial part of adolescence. We began to look for young adult (YA) literature that illustrates these pressures and found myriad wonderful books that clearly demonstrate how girls, both in the past and in the present, have struggled to develop a voice even while buffeted by harsh forces that try to stifle it. We found, through class discussions, that we could easily bring those issues to the surface and that girls were eager to investigate them. Using YA literature seemed a perfect way to help girls share and understand what they were experiencing in their daily lives.

This book, then, has grown out of our readings, experiences, and conversations with girls and their teachers and our discovery of the importance of weaving literature about girls' issues into the school curriculum. Now we wish to share our findings in a way that they can be of practical value. We have experimented with the ideas in these pages as part of the language arts or English classroom and as after-school activities. We have also talked with teachers who are doing the same things, and we have read about many others' experiences. We believe that literature-based discussion—sparked by group readings of books with female protagonists—is a powerful way to help girls think about the many developmental changes and outside influences they face between the ages of 10 and 16.

Organization of This Book

We have organized the book in a way that we think will be helpful to teachers. First, we review the issue of adolescent development, particularly as it applies to girls today. We explore the types of programs that have been developed to respond to current concerns about girls. Next, we propose a structure for examining literature to foster discussion and introduce dialogue about girls' development. To provide concrete examples, we review the various genres including the contemporary "problem novel," historical fiction, and fantasy and science fiction for their potential contributions to the examination of girls' issues. We view these genres through the lens of teachers and media specialists who are looking for specific texts to teach. Throughout the text, we specify both certain works that demonstrate our ideas and key concepts that can apply to any novel. We conclude the book by suggesting specific methods that teachers can use if they wish to incorporate discussions about girls' literature into their schools—namely, conducting either an extracurricular book club or literature circles during English or reading classes.

We are aware that the issues girls face parallel those that adolescent boys experience. Recently, we have begun to see articles and books that explore some of the problems faced by boys, and we believe that literature can and should provide vehicles for boys to explore their developmental issues. Although this book has been written with a focus on girls, it could easily be adapted to foster discussions concerning boys' issues. In fact, if books for girls are presented in a mixed-sex group, the discussion will inevitably lead to questions about and comparisons of girls' development to boys' development. This is an added benefit of introducing these books in classrooms.

We hope *Discovering Their Voices* will become a resource for reading and English language arts teachers like us who realize that many adolescent girls are at risk, yet have no forum to discuss what is happening to them. In addition to giving teachers specific ideas about how the create those forums, we hope this book will spark new strategies and approaches to be shared.

ACKNOWLEDGMENTS

THIS BOOK is about girls who are fighting to establish a voice. It has been inspired by the wonderful girls we have come to know in our classrooms and in our own families. We know how hard it is for them at times to speak out about what they believe, and we know what crushing pressures they are under to say what they think we—and others—want to hear.

From Marsha

I am especially indebted to my daughter, Dagny Sprague Landis, for sharing her ideas about so many of these issues, and for doing several edits of this manuscript. As a new English teacher, she is carrying the torch. I am thankful to my nieces Kelly Barnett and Devon Sprague, who shared with me many of their adolescent experiences and who became wonderful role models for other girls; to their mothers Lisa Barnett and Pat Sprague, who gracefully nurtured their unique voices; and for my own mother, Shirley Makibbin, who long ago established a wonderful voice that called many young women to teaching and to literature. I also owe a great debt to my husband Al, who has always encouraged me to speak up, even if he has heard what I'm saying many times before. Thanks to Markie Burch, Curly Johnson, and Rebecca Wheeler for their support and practical advice on moving the manuscript along, and for friends Sara and Pete Crumpacker who shared their knowledge and love of book clubs. Thanks to those wonderful teachers, Paul Lawrence and Lori Risher, who provided models for book chapters—and to new teachers Kyle Lumsden and Valerie Smith who created lessons just for the book. Lastly, I am so grateful for my collaborator, Kara Keeling, who has such a love and wealth of knowledge of young adult literature and was willing to share it all.

From Kara

I am first indebted to my parents, who jumpstarted my love of literature by reading to me, taking me to the library, suggesting more books for me to read, and gradually turning our house into a small library of much-loved books during my childhood and adolescence. Because of their support I always knew studying literature was a worthwhile focus for my life. I particularly value Mary Burgan, my department chair and dissertation director in graduate school, for modeling how much a woman who knows her mind and speaks it freely can achieve. I am thankful for my colleagues in the Children's Literature Association who continually introduce me to new books and new ways to think about older books. Thanks must also go to the students in my children's and young adult literature classes at Christopher Newport University, who have freely shared their ideas, enthusiasms, and criticisms about the books we have studied. I am grateful beyond words to my husband, Scott Pollard, for his patience and love, and for the ongoing conversations we have had about literature since the day we met. And finally, I have the greatest admiration and gratitude for my collaborator Marsha Sprague, whose tireless energy, optimism, and drive to make a difference in the lives of young people through the literature that excited her was the wellspring of this book.

From Both Authors

We could not have finished this book without the support of our academic department and administration. We both received grants, including precious time, from the Dean of the College of Liberal Arts of Christopher Newport University, Douglas Gordon, who is also a passionate lover of literature. The former chair of our department, Scott Pollard, was invaluable in helping us schedule our time and classes so that we could work on the book. We also appreciate the support we have received from our current chair, Tracey Schwarze, as we finished the manuscript.

Finally, we are greatly indebted to Tori Bachman and the editorial staff of the International Reading Association for their thoughtful and careful editing of this text.

CHAPTER 1

From *Fifteen* to *Speak*: Challenges Facing the Adolescent Girl in U.S. Society

ADOLESCENCE IS a developmental passage that has been widely recognized and extensively studied. Between the ages of 10 and 16, children experience rapid physical and emotional growth and change and engage in formative tasks that, if successfully completed, result in their entrance into adulthood (Erickson, 1950/1993). Erickson argues that the primary role of adolescence is to create an identity, thus avoiding role confusion. This prepares the young adult for the next task, which is to achieve intimacy with another. Erickson explains that the search for identity may cause the adolescent to "overidentify, to the point of apparent complete loss of identity, with the heroes of cliques and crowds" (p. 262). This search for identity pressures teens to try desperately to fit in, to be accepted as part of a crowd, and to reject (often cruelly) others who might threaten the sense of cohesion felt by a group. This summarizes, for most of us, our general understanding of adolescence: a search for who we are, for where we fit. We all can remember being afraid of wearing the wrong clothes or saying the wrong things throughout our teenage years. We often recall with embarrassment our yearning for (or in rare cases, celebration of) the status of being a popular kid.

What Girls Experience During Adolescence

The experiences of girls who enter and go through adolescence have been meticulously studied by psychologists. Some of the earliest research on this subject, which attempted to explore the experiences of girls as they entered adolescence, was conducted by Gilligan and colleagues as part of the Harvard Project on Women's Psychology and Girls' Development (Gilligan, Lyons, & Hammer, 1990). After an initial study conducted at a New York boarding school in the early 1980s, the researchers turned their attention to a private day school, the Laurel School for Girls in Cleveland, Ohio. Spanning the years from 1986 to 1990, this second study by Brown and Gilligan (1992) used two methods to explore the developmental processes of primarily affluent, white young women attending this school: First, a typical psychological interview presented hypothetical situations to the subjects and asked them for responses; then a more open-ended interview asked the girls to describe their thoughts and feelings. The girls were interviewed during the first, fourth, seventh, and tenth grades. Because it was a long-term study, all the girls could be tracked over time. Brown and Gilligan concluded that as girls go through adolescence they lose their inner voice—their sense of self. Girls tend to "dismiss their experience and modulate their voices.... For girls at adolescence to say what they are feeling and thinking often means to risk, in the words of many girls, losing their relationships and finding themselves powerless and alone" (Brown & Gilligan, 1992, p. 217). The researchers found that at 11 or 12, girls speak out and are honest about their thoughts and feelings, but they learn to silence themselves shortly after this age. This silencing occurred even when girls were, by standard psychological and academic measures, highly successful.

The problems that girls experience during adolescence catapulted into the public eye with the publication of Pipher's *Reviving Ophelia: Saving the Selves of Adolescent Girls* (1994). Pipher, writing from her firsthand experience as a counselor, describes what she perceives as an alarming malaise in adolescent girls. Echoing Brown and Gilligan, Pipher argues that girls entering adolescence experience a diminishing sense of who they are and what they can do. This, Pipher feels, is largely the result of messages that they receive from adults, the media, and their peers. Many girls react to these messages by withdrawing and effacing their passions at great cost to themselves. Others rebel by engaging in risk-taking behaviors such as drug and alcohol abuse and sexual experimentation. Some, desperately seeking to conform to unrealistic expectations, become anorexic or bulimic. Other girls, in despair, cut or mutilate their bodies. In her book, Pipher presents clients' case studies as examples of the thoughts and actions of girls enduring horrific experiences. One of her 15-year-old clients says flatly, "I've had trouble you can't imagine" (Pipher, 1994, p. 48). The book forced parents, teachers, and counselors to imagine the problems that many adolescent girls experience. The question was whether this was typical for most adolescent girls or just for those who ended up in a counselor's office.

The answer to that question may be found in *Ophelia Speaks: Adolescent Girls Write About Their Search for Self* by Sara Shandler (1999), who was 16 when she read *Reviving Ophelia*. She immediately connected to the voices of Pipher's girls. Despite being a high achiever and generally "happy and healthy adolescent girl" (p. xv), Shandler recognized that she had experienced many of the thoughts and feelings of Pipher's clients. She began asking for written reactions from her friends and found that they, too, were experiencing anguish that was largely hidden under a facade of normality. Shandler then began formally soliciting responses and writings from adolescent girls across the United States, and she received 815 contributions "from different religious, racial, and economic backgrounds, from small towns to large cities, in every major geographical area" (p. xv). Shandler selected from these entries those that exemplified girls' pain concerning their bodies and body images, their families, their friends, and their sexual identities and experiences, and other challenges such as academics, race, and depression. The writings confirm Pipher's portraits of girls as people who are undergoing tremendous pressures and traumatic experiences, rarely having the opportunity to talk about what is happening and terrified of being reviled if they do.

Because of the veil of silence that adolescent girls assume to protect themselves, it is difficult to find an agreement among statistics of drug and alcohol use, suicide attempts, eating disorders, and so on that they experience. One report suggests that, compared to boys, adolescent girls experience greater stress, are twice as likely to be depressed, and are much more as likely to attempt suicide (Rothenberg, 1997). In the United States, girls under 15 are five times more likely to give birth than female teens in other industrialized nations (Brumberg,

3

1998). In the 1997 Commonwealth Fund Survey of 3,532 high school girls and boys, reported by Johnson and Roberts (1999), over 20% of the girls said they had been physically or sexually abused; 23% had experienced depressive symptoms in the two weeks prior to the survey. Data gathered in 2002 (Anorexia Nervosa and Related Eating Disorders, Inc., n.d.) reveal that 1–4% of girls exhibit clinical anorexia nervosa or bulimia, and a far greater number experience disordered eating habits such as binge eating, extremely restrictive dieting, fasting, laxative abuse, or vomiting. Certainly, the statistics are distressing. Many, many adolescent girls are in trouble, and unless they participate in some type of supportive, open dialogue, they have no way to understand how to overcome the pressures of adolescence—let alone how to find their authentic self despite such pressures.

Literature That Illustrates Adolescent Girls' Experiences

One way of understanding what has changed in U.S. society regarding adolescent girls in the last half of the 20th century is to compare Beverly Cleary's *Fifteen* (1956/2003) to Laurie Halse Anderson's *Speak* (2003). The two novels, both centered on the experiences of high school girls, reveal dramatic changes in the social fabric of the United States from the mid-1950s to the end of the 20th century, particularly in the ways that adolescent girls come of age. There are so many parallels in the books that it appears that Anderson could have written *Speak* as a dark companion reader to *Fifteen*.

We learn the central character's name, Jane Purdy, in the first sentence of *Fifteen*. This early candor sets the tenor of the book: Everything is transparent, and there are very few secrets. We know all about Jane's thoughts and wishes because the author clearly reveals them to us. The third sentence informs the reader of Jane's preoccupation throughout the book: "Today I'm going to meet a boy" (p. 1). Indeed, Jane does meet a boy, Stan. He is handsome, pleasant, appealing, and slightly older than Jane. Like Jane, he comes from a white, middle class family. The book traces their burgeoning romance, which goes smoothly, barring a few hitches. First, Stan does not ask Jane to the first school dance because he has already invited an old girlfriend from his former school. Unfortunately, he does not tell Jane this information until after the dance, but finally he explains and all is forgiven. Second, Stan has an unexpected appendectomy, which puts him out of the picture for a while but ultimately allows Jane to declare her feelings for him and actually makes their relationship stronger. The book ends with Jane and Stan "going steady," which has been Jane's goal all along.

Like Jane and Stan, the other characters in the book are also white, middle class, and pleasant. Jane's mother and father (her father's occupation is unspecified, but her mother is a stay-at-home mom) are devoted to Jane and are very protective of her. Jane's mother insists that Jane wear clothes that are somewhat childish, and Jane's father teases her about her boyfriend. They provide some of the gentle humor that is found throughout the book. Jane's best friend, Julie, is totally supportive of Jane and very much like her; they run a baby-sitting service together. The only moderately unpleasant character is a girl in their class named Marcy, who is popular, self-absorbed, and arrogant. The book does have a theme of sorts: Jane realizes that when she tries to act like Marcy, she makes both her friends and herself miserable. When she acts like herself (nice and friendly), she is happy. Author Cleary sums up this concept: "She would remember she was Jane Purdy and no one else. Maybe she was doing the wrong thing, but that was the way she was" (p. 176).

The contrast between *Fifteen* and *Speak* cannot be starker. Both books open with girls who are getting ready to go back to school. However, while Jane is looking forward to it, *Speak*'s central character, Melinda, is dreading it. We do not know Melinda's name until page 24 of the novel. We only know that something is very wrong in Melinda's life because her good friends from the previous school year will not speak to her. We find out on page 27 that Melinda "called the cops" during a summer party. Gradually we learn that Melinda harbors a secret that is making her withdrawn and depressed: She was raped at the summer party but has been unable to tell anyone about it. Unlike Jane Purdy, luckily endowed with a supporting cast of characters, Melinda is alone. Her parents, both of whom work, seem unable or unwilling to acknowledge the depth of Melinda's despair. Her best friend, Rachel, has turned on her after the cop-calling incident, and the rest of her middle school friends are simply ignoring her. Melinda does meet a new "friend," Heather, but Heather ultimately betrays Melinda in her attempts to become part of a clique. The central boy in Melinda's life is the boy who raped her. Seldom calling the perpetrator by name, Melinda refers to him as "IT." This depersonalization is an attempt to objectify her traumatic experience. Melinda's nerdy biology lab partner, David, is a possible male counter to "IT." He expresses an interest in being Melinda's friend, but Melinda has difficulty connecting to anyone because of her rape.

The theme of the book centers on Melinda's loss of identity because of the trauma she has endured. She slowly loses the ability to speak as she sinks deeper and deeper into despair. She is saved from complete annihilation by two things: (1) an art teacher who challenges her to express her feelings through art, and (2) a message she writes on a bathroom wall that warns other girls of "IT." These actions give Melinda the courage to tell her former best friend Rachel about her experience, and although at first Rachel does not believe her, Melinda becomes empowered by the event. At the end of the novel, "IT" attempts to rape Melinda again. This time, however, she has the ability to scream and to fight back. Although dark, *Speak* offers frequent, biting moments of sarcastic humor through Melinda's descriptions of her teachers and the cliques that exist at her high school.

What These Novels Reflect

These two books show the challenges that adolescent girls have faced for generations. The expectation of the adolescent girl, as reflected in *Fifteen*, is that she will adhere to the commandments of society, winning a male who will fulfill the role of decision maker and provider. Such a female role was well-established in the United States in 1956. Generally, mothers were expected to remain at home to provide guidance, support, and unconditional love for their children. Fathers—at least those of the middle class—contributed to the financial security of a household that sheltered young women from financial worries.

It was expected that young men would respect young ladies and protect their innocence. Many girls were raised in neighborhoods or towns in which the inhabitants knew them and contributed to their senses of security and protection.

Certainly this idyllic picture has major flaws. We know now that during 1950s many men, old and young, abused and disrespected women and girls. Women, constrained to restrictive roles, sometimes became suicidal and alcoholic. Young girls rebelled and became promiscuous. The feminist movement of the 1960s and 1970s sought to liberate women by encouraging them to seek new roles and establish gender equity. Unfortunately, the corollary changes in society have caused a new set of challenges for girls. As Pipher points out,

> Traditionally parents have wondered what their teens are doing, but now teens are much more likely to be doing things that can get them killed....The protected place in space and time that we once called childhood has grown shorter. (1994, p. 28)

For many of the girls in the United States today, there are few protective systems in place. In modern families, mothers often are working outside the home, and their children are not the sole focus of their lives. In *Speak*, Melinda's mother is too stressed and distracted by work to deal with Melinda's increasing problems. Many girls in the United States do not have a father in the home for a large part of their lives because more than half of all marriages end in divorce. This means that girls have experienced a loss of financial and emotional security. As for teenage boys "respecting" a girl's body, Pipher quotes a "recent study in Rhode Island" (p. 206) that shows that more than half of the teens questioned (both males and females) believed that forced sex was justified if the girl had "led the guy on" (p. 206). Finally, there is very little sense of community in modern cities and towns; the rise of urban sprawl and mammoth suburbs has created neighborhoods of strangers who do not even speak to one another.

In Jane Purdy's day, teenage girls were expected to be pretty, sweet, and loveable. The role of Kitten on the television program *Father Knows Best* (the title is exemplary of the era) typified the eager, pleasant young woman society required. This placed unrealistic and suffocating demands on many high-spirited, intelligent young women of the time, forcing them to repress their abilities and aspirations.

And what is the young woman of today supposed to be? Because of the pervasive influences of television, fashion magazines, and movies, today's teen is expected to fulfill all of the following roles: sex kitten, waif, seductress, fashion model, athlete, scholar, and aspiring homemaker. It is too much for many girls, who withdraw into depression, drug abuse, and even suicide as they give up trying to achieve the behaviors expected of them with little support and no safety nets.

Fifteen and *Speak* are fascinating novels to explore in terms of the dilemmas faced by both girls in the 1950s and girls in the 1990s. Read together, these books reveal real changes in the world that now envelops adolescent girls.

What the Scholars Say About Girls' Experiences in Schools

It is not surprising that school's role in the lives of girls has been scrutinized. After all, girls spend almost as many waking hours in school as at home. Beginning in the early 1970s, a number of researchers explored the effects of sexism in schools and society. In 1995, the American Association of University Women (AAUW) Educational Foundation commissioned a report that synthesized research on adolescent girls in schools. The report, titled *How Schools Shortchange Girls*, summarizes devastating findings on the loss of self-esteem and decline of academic achievement experienced by many adolescent females. Sadker and Sadker (1994) explored a number of areas, using statistical studies as well as interviews, to show what happens to girls over the course of their years in school. Their book, *Failing at Fairness: How Our Schools Cheat Girls*, documents girls' feelings about their bodies and their minds and how these feelings spiral downward during middle and high school. Sadker and Sadker report the response of thousands of students to the prompt, "Suppose you woke up tomorrow and found you were a member of the other sex. How would your life be different?" (p. 83). In general, girls were intrigued by the idea of being a boy, while boys found it "appalling, disgusting, and humiliating" to think about becoming female (p. 83). The authors report on the tendency of girls to be ignored by both male and female teachers in the public school classroom and the continuation of this practice in colleges and universities. The book cites troubling statistics about campus rape and sexual harassment in school buildings. One chapter is devoted to academic score discrepancies between boys and girls, particularly in the areas of mathematics and science. It acknowledges the superior achievement of girls on report cards, attributing it to socialized conforming behaviors that result in better grades but less learning. It is possible that the Sadker and Sadker book would have drawn more attention if it had not been eclipsed by the publication of Pipher's *Reviving Ophelia* the same year, which was heavily marketed and sold in commercial bookstores.

The AAUW Educational Foundation issued a second report in 1994, the same year that *Failing at Fairness* was published. This report, *Hostile Hallways: The AAUW Survey on Sexual Harassment in America's Schools* (1993), details the sexual harassment endured by adolescent girls in schools, revealing that 8 out of 10 students, mostly female, experienced some form of sexual harassment at school, including the spreading of rumors and unwanted touching. A third AAUW report, *Girls in the Middle: Working to Succeed in Schools* (Cohen & Blanc, 1996), examines the ways that middle school girls cope with the difficult challenges of adolescence. One such way is to speak out, or assert oneself. One role that girls assume is the "maverick leader," the girl who loudly speaks out, competes for grades and attention, and is usually effective in handling school. On the other hand, the "troublemaker" seeks attention by confronting authority and breaking the rules (p. 17). A second way is "doing school," which means conforming to what is expected (p. 17). This method produces both the "schoolgirl," who conforms to all expectations, is well behaved in school, and makes good grades, and the "play schoolgirl," who merely feigns compliance to get away with other, less appropriate behaviors. A third method of negotiating school is to cross borders. By doing so, a girl can belong to or fit in with various groups in the school. The "schoolgirl/cool girl" is somewhat aloof and selects behaviors that will work to her advantage, while the "translator" is able to discern the need for different behaviors based on different settings and can cross lines of race and culture to succeed in various roles (p. 17). The vitality of roles to success in adolescence is also explored in Orenstein's *Schoolgirls: Young Women, Self-Esteem, and the Confidence Gap* (1994), a qualitative study of the behaviors of girls in three California middle schools. Orenstein documents the ways in which girls try to cope with the pressures on them: Some become "schoolgirls" but others are cast as "sluts"; some engage in binging or cutting as a way to deal with their anxieties. Both books show how difficult it is for girls to maintain their sense of adequacy and self.

Girls in the Middle (Cohen & Blanc, 1996) offers a look at the ways different types of schools address issues of gender. Suburban schools "tended to define gender issues in terms of challenges to be met through policy and program initiatives" such as sexual harassment policies (p. 39). Urban schools "tended to define gender issues in the context of the many challenges facing low-income, minority youngsters—both male and female" (p. 40). In these urban schools, adults tried to connect with young people on a personal level and provide support to them. In the last category, rural schools, the report found that the issue of gender was approached "indirectly"; the schools tried to maintain typical gender roles while assisting girls in developing strengths (such as independence) that would help them prepare for adulthood (p. 40). The report concludes with specific suggestions of actions that all schools could adopt to assist girls in overcoming the challenges of adolescence. Major recommendations include the following:

1. Expand the range of acceptable behaviors for girls, particularly "nonconforming" behaviors such as argumentation and assertion.

2. Create a mentor program for girls and support adult mentors through funding and recognition.

3. Build identity development into the school curriculum. Provide opportunities for girls and boys to explore and discuss gender issues.

4. Foster opportunities for girls to assume leadership positions within both school and classroom settings.

5. Examine and share with area schools current practices of handling gender issues.

6. Make gender equity a school priority.

7. Create public forums to address the issue of gender equity.

8. Conduct research on gender issues.

The National Council of Teachers of English (NCTE) has long recognized the lack of gender equity in the English/Language Arts curriculum. In particular, they have noted the preponderance of literature focused on male protagonists. In 1975, a position statement on the importance of gender equity in literature was produced by the Women's Assembly of NCTE under the leadership of Aileen Pace Nielson. This statement offered a list of books that were deemed beneficial for girls as well as ideas for how teachers could use the books. This position statement has been updated and is now available as *Guidelines for a Gender-Balanced Curriculum in English* in two versions, one for teachers of pre-K to grade 6 and one for teachers of grades 7–12. The material, prepared by the Women in Literature and Life Assembly (WILLA) of the NCTE, is available and accessible through the NCTE website (www.ncte.org).

School and Community Programs to Foster Girls' Identities

So what has been the school and community response to the problems highlighted in this research? Literature written since 1994 reports the existence of a number of programs that aim for the successful development of adolescent girls. Many appear to be one-time efforts conducted mainly for the purpose of research, rather than sustained reform initiatives. However, the programs are interesting and represent possible models for success. They can be divided into programs that address strengthening self-esteem; academics, including single-sex classrooms; or literature/reading activities. The following pages describe a few of the programs in each category.

Programs That Focus on Self-Esteem

Because of a variety of concerns from both faculty members and female students, a team of teachers and an administrator developed a program for girls at Benjamin Tasker Middle School in Bowie, Maryland (Hood, 1994). The program was open to seventh-grade girls and then carried over into the eighth grade. The program had six goals:

1. to provide positive learning experiences for young girls;
2. to teach social skills and conflict management to enhance self-esteem and self-efficacy;
3. to provide current information about female issues;
4. to provide opportunities for dialog, role modeling, and mentoring;
5. to empower adolescent females while helping them value interdependence through leadership training; and
6. to promote multicultural relationships and bonding. (Hood, 1994, pp. 24–25)

To accomplish these goals, girls attended small-group meetings and special assemblies. In small-group meetings, girls engaged in discussion, participated in cooperative projects such as making a video, wrote and shared journals, learned about family histories, and participated in social skills training. Although no specific data was reported, the authors declared the program beneficial for students, parents, teachers, and administrators. Unfortunately, a call to the school in January of 2000 indicated that the program no longer existed.

University researchers also have designed several intervention programs for adolescent girls. Lucas (1999) instituted a mentoring program for sixth-grade girls at three middle schools in New Hampshire. Her purpose was to conduct a research study that investigated the relationships between undergraduate mentors and the middle schoolers over the course of the study, and to determine how these relationships changed over time. Lucas was particularly interested in the psychological context of the relationships, focusing on the structural developmental stages of mentors and mentees. In the program there were 31 mentor-mentee pairs at the three middle schools. Ten pairs were selected for in-depth analysis. The mentors met once a week after school with the middle school students throughout a school year.

During the meetings, the group engaged in whole-group activities, some small-group activities, and dyad (mentor-mentee) activities. Activities included cooking, craft making, having informal discussions, and sharing schoolwork. The mentor was available to help with homework and act as a tutor but could also participate in craft making and other activities. (It is not clear why cooking and crafts, traditionally female activities, were selected.) The researcher's analysis indicated that the mentoring activity produced a series of processes: "(1) valuing each other's role; (2) taking on complementary roles; (3) identifying with one another; (4) sharing in a variety of activities; (5) experiencing turning points; (6) demonstrating affection for one another" (Lucas, 1999, p. 23). Lucas found that the rate and extent of these processes varied with each dyad. Her conclusion was that mentoring relationships could be enriching for both parties but that time and the support of facilitators was important.

A summer program far removed from the school or university setting is the Connecting With Courage (CWC) program for girls ages 12 and 13, developed by Outward Bound school at Thompson Island, Massachusetts (Porter, 1996). CWC is a 14-day course, which is much longer than other Outward Bound programs. In addition, girls are welcome to complete the course with their friends, a practice discouraged in most Outward Bound programs. However, the Outward Bound tenets of experiential learning and courageous risk-taking are at the heart of this program as well. Porter reports that the CWC program combines artistic, creative elements with traditional outdoor activities. For instance, the course might include backpacking, rock climbing, and a ropes course, but the girls might also make friendship bracelets or create a mural. Another important part of the program is talking about relationships, being female, and finding one's own voice with which to speak out. Although no formal evaluation of the program is reported, Porter states, "For the three years since its inception, demand and numbers of courses offered have risen exponentially.... The rapid growth of this program is proof that it meets important personal needs while breaking tradition" (p. 272). At the time of this book's publication, the program is still offered each summer for groups of girls ages 12 to 13 ("2006 Outward Bound Summer Expeditions," 2006).

Programs That Focus on Mathematics and Science

The Voices of Girls in Science, Math and Technology program was funded by the National Science Foundation and developed by the Appalachia Educational Lab (Carter, 1997). Sixty-five middle school students from rural and urban settings participated in a three-year program. The goals of the project were to increase girls' capacities and confidence in their ability to do well in science, mathematics, and technology. During the first year of the project, sixth-grade girls were involved in Saturday workshops in which they studied science, mathematics, and technology within the context of the Appalachian culture. For example, during one workshop girls studied the mathematics of designing quilts. They also designed websites for their school and engaged in a simulation of a space voyage. During the second year, the students (now seventh graders) continued attending the workshops and field trips, but in addition they were assigned adult mentors who worked in the scientific and technical fields. The girls collaborated with their mentors on scientific investigations. In the third year, now as eighth graders, the girls worked as "virtual scientists" and also became role models for elementary school students. In addition, tutorial sessions helped the girls gain study skills and effectively review what they had learned. A study of program participants in urban versus rural settings (Carter, 1997) indicated that the program seemed to have more impact on rural girls than urban girls.

Hudson and Stiles (1998) summarize a number of studies that have been done on single-sex learning environments. Almost all these studies have focused on girls' improved ability to perform well in mathematics and science when placed in single-sex settings. For example, Perry found that "grade-point averages for both girls and boys were higher in single-sex mathematics and science classes than in mixed-gender classes at a Virginia middle school" (cited in Hudson & Stiles, 1998, p. 57). A pilot program in a San Francisco middle school also reported improved academic achievement as well as increased participation of students in lessons in single-sex classes (Harrison, cited in Hudson & Stiles, 1998, p. 58). Also, a series of workshops for seventh-grade girls, designed to address issues of gender stereotyping and fears about sexual harassment, has "helped reverse a slide in...standardized math and science scores" (Gillis, cited in Hudson & Stiles, 1998, p. 58). According to Gillis, truancy at that school also has decreased.

It is worthwhile to note that Bailey (1996) cautions against the institution of single-sex classes as a solution to gender inequity. She writes,

> Removing girls from classes in order to provide better learning opportunities for them can imply that girls and boys are so different that they must be taught in radically different ways. When all-girl classes are set up specifically in science or math, an underlying, if unintended, message can be that girls are less capable in these subjects. (p. 76)

In addition, Bailey argues that Title IX, enacted in 1972 (U.S. Department of Labor, n.d.), permits single-sex instruction only in limited situations (specifically, in classes dealing with human sexuality or in sports that involve bodily contact). Her contention is that girls must learn to hold their own in the classroom and that schools and teachers can help them do so.

Programs That Focus on Literacy

Smith (1997) initiated an after-school book club as a way to engage middle school girls in a large northeastern city. Eight sixth-grade girls joined the club and met for 17 sessions during a nine-month period. The girls read four novels that were selected by both the girls and the researcher from "award-winning young adult fiction that presented a variety of strong female characters who challenge the status quo" (p. 2). According to the researcher's analysis, the book club provided a safe environment for girls to explore issues that were important to them and also gave them a springboard to talk about these issues. For example, one girl was able to discuss her father's death and the difficulty that she had sharing it with friends. The researcher also felt that students could explore their own identities in regards to race and culture in the book club.

Heilman and Goodman (1996) targeted a K–12 school in a midwestern city that offered exploratory courses to students on a monthly rotation. The researchers initiated an elective course in gender identity, in which upper elementary, middle, and high school students examined the role of women in media and film. Based on student response, they also extended the exploration to children's literature. Finally, the students created personal narratives about their own experiences with gender identity and then studied their narratives to uncover major themes. The instructors reported that the students who enrolled responded positively to the course content. Although there was definite resistance in the school to the course, particularly on the part of male students, the authors concluded that the study of gender identity was a crucial part of an effective high school curriculum.

Analysis of These Programs

It is clear that most of the specific programs reported above have been the result of research studies or university programs that often represent one-time interventions. Unfortunately, the school-based programs were short-lived, citing changes in administration and personnel as reasons for their discontinuations. It is disturbing that none of the programs show systematic efforts on the part of a school or school system to engage in meaningful efforts to address the problems of girls so clearly evidenced by the studies of the 1990s.

This phenomenon has been confirmed by our own observations and surveys of schools in our region as well (see Sprague, 2003, for more information). To our knowledge, few schools offer specific programs targeted to girls—and the programs that are offered usually are transitory. Furthermore, several programs we have observed offer "etiquette classes" in which at-risk girls are taught manners and engage in service activities. This element of the clubs appears to emphasize conformity as the key to success, a societal message harmful to the developing adolescent girl. It is almost a return to the 1950s, seeking to restrict girls to a role of compliance and subservience. Even the emphasis on service clubs for girls is suspect unless there are boys' clubs that are also engaged in service activities. It implies that women are the logical choice for caregivers and nurturers, again reinforcing old stereotypes.

Summary

Our research has confirmed what we suspected: Despite studies and statistics indicating the difficulties faced by girls, few schools have adopted programs that address the developmental needs of adolescent girls. Some of the academic programs that we learned about are targeted to increasing girls' performance in schools—a worthy goal, but one we question as perhaps inadvertently increasing the pressure that girls feel. For instance, teen author Shandler (1999) writes about the cost of doing well in school, as her peers describe "[their] constant stretch toward scholastic perfection, or at least betterment, and [their] unyielding dissatisfaction with the results" (p. 224). Some of the programs that we looked at relied on grant money, almost guaranteeing a short shelf life. Our question, then, as a former English language arts teacher and an English professor, was, How could we use the rich world of literature (as a few of our predecessors had attempted) to build discussions of gender identity and girls' issues into classrooms and schools? Every school's curriculum contains time designated to spend on books. We began to look for ways to structure that effort, and the next chapter outlines how we approached this task.

CHAPTER 2

How to Use Literature to Explore Adolescent Girls' Developmental Issues

A S DISCUSSED in the previous chapter, many adolescent girls are at risk for low self-esteem, poor academic performance, depression, self-mutilation, sexual and physical abuse, and even suicide. Despite a clear call for action, the response of schools has been surprisingly muted. Of most practical importance to teachers is the recommendation from the American Association of University Women (AAUW) for teachers of adolescents: "Open dialogue on gender issues in the classroom. Discuss gender as an aspect of students' lives, curricular materials, and classroom dynamics... Use curricula and materials that show females and males from various cultures in a variety of roles" (Cohen & Blanc, 1996, p. 88). This stance is supported by the National Council of Teachers of English's (NCTE; 1990a) position statements on a gender-balanced curriculum: "Teachers can be instrumental in helping students reflect on gendered expectations. Teachers can challenge those expectations by showing options and alternatives so readers seek to confront the inequities they find in their own lives" (para. 4).

As Gilligan and her colleagues (1990) so clearly relate, the task of the adolescent girl is to find and remain true to her inner self—to avoid being co-opted by societal and peer expectations into assuming a false identity. In the typical upper elementary, middle, and high school curriculum, there is little opportunity for girls (or boys) to study and discuss the reality of what happens to them during adolescence and what forces are at work during that time. To adults who care about nurturing girls' development and allowing both boys and girls to explore the issues involved, this is a disservice. How, then, can this discussion be initiated? A logical solution is to explore the curriculum of reading and literature.

How Can Literature Help Adolescent Girls?

Nowhere is the opportunity for dialogue about adolescence greater than in the study of literature. A number of novels written in the past 10–15 years directly address the issues of girls' development through various plot devices. Adler and Clark (1991) advocate the use of novels in addressing the development of adolescent girls. While recognizing the limitations of literature in solving psychological problems, they reference Spache (1978, as cited in Adler & Clark, p. 578): "It is through facilitated discussion that readers recognize that they are not the first to meet and solve problems, become aware of previously unrecognized problems, and find solutions without experiencing feelings of inferiority, guilt, fear or shame." Even when discussions result in the realization that there are no simple solutions for problems, they may help adolescent girls to develop a more authentic sense of who they are in the context of their culture.

McCracken (1992) presents an intensive look at how English language arts teachers can raise awareness of gender issues through their selection and discussion of literature by and about women and highlights the ways in which discussion of texts through the lens of gender can help young women as "the girls are given space to express their feelings" (p. 64). Stover (1992) describes a number of books that teachers can use to have students "explore how their own gender influences their response to writings by men and women" (p. 103). Stover argues that teachers need to select texts that provide strong models, both male and female, in furthering what Rosenblatt (1938, cited in Stover) offers as a gift of literature: "Through books the reader may explore his [or her] own nature, become aware of potentialities for thought and feeling within himself [or herself], acquire clearer perspective and develop aims and a new sense of direction" (p. 106).

Whaley and Dodge (1999) report success in maintaining an elective high school course in women's literature for over 21 years. Issues of gender are embedded within that curriculum, as delineated in the stated purpose of the course:

> To provide participants with models of women from a wide spectrum of society who have struggled to free themselves from traditional roles and who have come to recognize that the modern woman must merge her inner and outer selves in order to become wholly human. (p. 194)

We heartily endorse the goal of having students learn about strong women. However, we would like to see *all* girls have a chance to confront their developmental issues, preferably beginning in upper elementary and middle school, which is when they encounter the first serious challenges to their identities. If literature is an appropriate vehicle for this confrontation, then what are the specific selections that would help girls understand and discuss the issues? And how do teachers identify the most appropriate novels to facilitate discussion?

Selecting Literature That Addresses Girls' Issues

A number of writers have examined the many books published that contain compelling female characters. Odean (1997) created a wonderful resource in *Great Books for Girls*, which presents a list of more than 600 books featuring strong girls, from picture books through young adult (YA) novels for readers ages 12–14. Odean writes,

> In selecting these books, I looked for girls and women who faced the world without timidity, either from the first or after overcoming their fears. I found female characters who are creative, capable, articulate, and intelligent. They solve problems, face challenges, resolve conflicts, and go on journeys. These girls are not waiting to be rescued; they are doing the rescuing. Nor are they waiting for a male to provide a happy ending: They are fashioning their own stories. (p. 4)

Odean sorts the books into a number of different categories such as sports stories, biographies, historical fiction, mysteries, science fiction, and fantasy.

Another excellent source for books that feature strong female characters is *100 Books for Girls to Grow On* (Dodson, 1998), which gives a brief summary of 100 books, organized alphabetically and intended for girls ages 9–13, followed by thought-provoking discussion questions meant to lead to central issues that girls need to tackle. For example, the discussion questions for *From the Mixed-Up Files of Mrs. Basil E. Frankweiler* (Konigsburg, 1967/1998), include the following:

- Claudia is "bored with being straight-A Claudia Kincaid." Why? What does Claudia want from life? Have you ever been labeled, or felt like you had to meet other people's expectations of you? (p. 86)
- Claudia says that she and Jamie complement each other perfectly. What does she mean? How do they become a team during their stay in the museum? Discuss the relationship they have, and how it changes during the book. (p. 87)

Dodson wrote this book as a supplement to her successful publication *The Mother-Daughter Book Club: How Ten Busy Mothers and Daughters Came Together to Talk, Laugh and Learn Through Their Love of Reading* (1997), which suggests ways in which girls and their mothers can read the same book and discuss it with other mother-daughter pairs.

Yet another resource book, *Once Upon a Heroine: 400 Books for Girls to Love* (Cooper-Mullin & Coye, 1998), not only provides a list of books but also contains entries by noted American females who recount their favorite childhood books. In addition, Cooper-Mullin and Coye extend the range of books into those aimed at students in high school.

The NCTE (1990a) guidelines mentioned earlier also provide lists of books with strong female characters, both for teachers of pre-K–6 and grades 7–12. In addition, they offer ways to discuss the books and additional resources that can help. Teachers, parents, media specialists, and others can use these rich resources to quickly identify books to use to examine girls' development. However, because many new books are published each year, and because there are some that have not yet been discovered by these authors, we have created a list of questions to use to determine if a book might foster productive dialogue. If, when examining a YA novel the answer to the following questions is "yes," that book certainly will be a candidate for use with students:

- Does the book feature a young female as a protagonist?
- Does the book place the girl in a position where she is being asked to conform to certain expected behaviors because she is female?
- Does the book illustrate forces that limit her choices, such as parents, societal expectations, or peer pressure?
- Does the book show the girl struggling against those forces?
- Does the girl define herself by the end of the book in ways that reflect her choices?

Framing the Discussion

These book lists are great resources for teachers who want to select books that can be focal points for discussion, and teachers will find many more books that can serve as discussion initiators in examining girls' issues. But what is to be discussed? Although the lists of questions offered by some of the authors are helpful in establishing a general understanding of the characters and the books, we want girls to understand the forces at work in shaping their development. Figure 1 represents a visual framework we created to help us target these features. This framework also can be shared with students while reading the books.

The Impact of Gender on Developing Voice

There are many forces that act upon and shape the construction of an identity, but one of the major forces is gender. Being male or female contributes certain features to identity because all societies attribute different characteristics to the male and female sexes. These societal expectations circumscribe the attributes, beliefs, and values that are acceptable for men and women. Of course, these societal expectations

Figure 1 Expression/Suppression Framework for Discussing Elements That Influence the Development of Voice

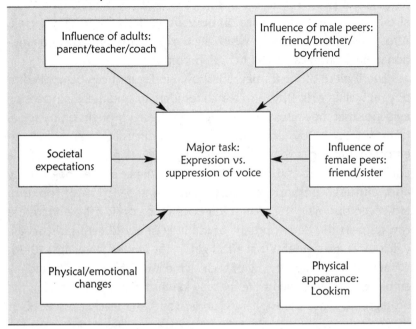

vary between different cultures and change over time. For example, in U.S. society women are expected to be their children's caregivers, so part of a woman's identity lies in the actions that nurture and sustain her offspring. More recently, women are also expected to contribute to the income of the household, so part of a woman's identity lies in her professional skills—and how well she balances work and home life.

In the identity construction of females, other factors come into play. We have tried to identify those in Figure 1. For example, despite the adolescent's typical rejection of parental control, those attitudes and values that have been expressed by parents are embedded in the adolescent's psyche, and many will become part of the adolescent's identity. Other adults such as teachers, coaches, grandparents, or aunts and uncles can be significant to the adolescent girl as well. Of course, peer influence is paramount in the development of girls' world views. Friends, boyfriends, sisters, and brothers all can affect a girl's willingness to speak out and might even determine what she is willing to say and do. In today's society, physical appearance and *lookism*, or the prejudice against people who are not physically attractive (Safire, 2000), also have dramatic influence on how an adolescent girl sees herself. Also, the way and timing in which a girl experiences physical and emotional maturation can affect her self-perception.

Every piece of the framework shown in Figure 1 can be applied to boys as well as girls. Boys also search for identity, and there is increasing evidence that they also are suffering from stresses brought on by societal expectations. Boys, too, can be helped by discussing the physical and emotional changes they experience, by analyzing the effects of the adults in their lives, and by examining the influence of their peers. They also, although perhaps to a lesser degree, are victims of lookism. However, our main purpose in this book is to consider how literature can support the development of identity of adolescent girls, so we will look at the elements that affect girls in the United States ages 10–16. What follows is an overview of each element in the framework and examples of books that illustrate the way in which that element affects the protagonist. Once the element is understood, the teacher can apply it to the analysis of any book and use the ideas for discussion.

Expression vs. Suppression of Voice

The center of Figure 1 shows what we believe to be the major task of girls in adolescence: to find and express their true voices. One could argue that this is the task of all adolescents. Psychologists refer to it as identity construction. According to Vignoles, Regaia, Manzi, Golledge, and Scabini (2006), identity is formed through "a complex interplay of cognitive, affective and social interaction processes, occurring within particular cultural and local contexts" (para. 4). Prior to entering adolescence, the child mimics his or her parents' beliefs and behaviors. If the parent says, "You are so funny," then the child accepts that label and acts accordingly. As the frontal lobe of the brain organizes during the preteen and early teenage years, however, the child begins to question the pronouncements of his or her parents and looks elsewhere for validation or refutation of parental values. Thus begins a long process of searching for one's own place in the world, often accompanied by outright rebellion and rejection of parental values. Through this process, the child forms his or her identity and finds his or her authentic voice.

What does that mean? Developing a voice means being able to answer the questions, Who am I? What do I believe? What do I value? and then act accordingly. For example, the ability to answer the question, Who am I? implies the capacity to self-analyze and recognize character traits: Am I loyal, stubborn, smart, funny? If I am loyal, what will I do when a friend is accused of something? In my true voice, I will defend my friend. The second question, What do I believe? addresses my relation to the world around me: Do I have religious and spiritual beliefs? Do I believe that all people are basically good? Do I believe that I can contribute to the world? If I hold true to my spiritual beliefs, I will pray and treat others with kindness and charity. Defining my beliefs will help me answer the question, What do I value? If I believe that people are basically good, then I value attempts to rehabilitate criminals, and I will support programs that do so. I might also value the earth and its resources; I could join an ecology club and go out and pick up litter. Being able to answer the questions, Who am I? What do I believe? What do I value? and act accordingly is at the core of identity construction.

Brown and Gilligan (1992) have done a great service documenting how girls' voices are silenced as they enter adolescence. One example they cite is a young girl who noticed that her parents were not listening to her during dinner. She fantasized about blowing a police whistle so her family would have to listen. Because girls learn that speaking out often causes dissension and unhappiness, they learn to withdraw rather than confront. Brown and Gilligan write,

> Girls at the edge of adolescence face a central relational crisis: to speak what they know through experience of themselves and of relationships creates political problems—disagreement with authorities, disrupting relationships—while not to speak leaves a residue of psychological problems: false relationships and confusion as to what they feel and think. (p. 214)

Examining a work of literature allows readers to recognize when a girl is expressing her voice. The characters in the texts we have selected learn to clearly express who they are, at least by the ends of the books. An excellent example is Cimorene, the protagonist of *Dealing with Dragons* (Wrede, 1990). Cimorene is a princess, yet she rejects the typical princess duties of dancing, sewing, and being rescued by princes. She does not want to marry the prince selected by her parents so she goes looking for a dragon to serve, instead of taking the more traditional route of being captured. The dragon, Woraug, is offended by her initiative:

> "No proper princess would come out looking for dragons," Woraug objected.
> "Well, I'm not a proper princess, then," Cimorene snapped. "I make cherries jubilee, and I volunteer for dragons, and I conjugate Latin verbs—or I would, if anyone would let me. So there!" (pp. 18–19)

Cimorene is well aware of her skills in academics and problem solving; in the book she finds a setting that requires these skills. She is able to articulate clearly her beliefs and values, and act on them.

As girls read literature, they can, in effect, blow a police whistle when female characters become silent rather than say what they think or act according to their beliefs. Girls can celebrate when these characters resist pressures to retreat rather than confront. Parents, teachers, and other concerned adults can encourage and teach girls to recognize when this silencing occurs both in literature and real life.

What is it that makes Cimorene and other strong literary females express or suppress their voices? Analyzing female characters using the following questions can reveal the forces that affect girls' suppression or expression of voice:

- **Who is the main character of this novel?**
- **What does she believe and value?**
- **Does she speak up for these things and act accordingly?**
- **What are her strengths and weaknesses?**
- **How is she like me? Different from me?**

The development of voice is actualized or impeded by a number of forces, which are symbolized by the boxes in the outer ring of Figure 1 (see page 23), and we will dissect each in the following sections.

Societal Expectations

The development of the modern role of women in Western culture is primarily a function of economics, according to a United Nations report (Michel, 1986) that claims that in the feudal system, prior to the 14th century, women were accorded the rights of managing property and representing themselves in court. However, with the end of the feudal system and the establishment of private property ownership, law codes reverted to the earlier Roman practice of labeling women *fragilitis sexus* (the weaker sex), and the husband became the "head and administrator of family property" (pp. 17–18). With no authority to make decisions or legally represent themselves, women had little say in their destinies.

In modern times, feminist authors, as well as psychologists and sociologists, have clearly articulated the roles expected of females in Western culture. As they point out, females are expected to be compliant, quiet, and well mannered. It has been demanded through much of modern history that a woman be subservient to men (first to a father and then to a husband) and that she will place marriage and raising children as top priorities in her life. Historically, women have been expected to remain in the home and to adopt tasks of cooking, cleaning, and sewing, instead of pursuing academics or athletics. During most years of so-called civilized society, women have not been able to own property or vote, and although these rights are now established in industrial societies, the stigma of women being incapable of managing people or finances still lingers. Women still earn far less than men do, and a female vice-president or president of the United States has yet to be elected. The historical and sociological perspective of the women's movement is barely explored in the middle or high school curriculum; if girls about learn it, they do so from their mothers or interested female teachers. Sadker and Sadker (1994) point out that less than 3% of a typical 1,000-page U.S. history textbook contains history about women, and only eight women have at least 25 lines devoted to them.

In fact, schools have unwittingly fostered the roles that U.S. society expects from its girls. Many studies have confirmed that teachers treat boys differently from girls. Sadker and Sadker (1994) have demonstrated that teachers not only call on boys far more often, but they also are likely to give boys many more suggestions for improvement, encourage them more, and spend more time with them. Sadly, this occurs even when the teacher is female (Leder, cited in Butler & Manning, 1998). The subconscious expectation is that the boy student might become an important politician or CEO, while it is less likely that the girl student will.

School textbooks have been studied extensively for their part in stereotyping girls. Only in the past 30 years have publishers been challenged on their portrayals of females in textbooks. Many women today were raised with readers depicting pretty, passive girls watching boys run and play. Girls were frequently portrayed as babysitters and eventually mothers; boys were portrayed as protectors and eventually breadwinners. Fortunately, most textbooks are now carefully evaluated for possible gender biases before they are adopted.

Portrayal of Societal Expectations in Young Adult Literature

How can girls understand which societal forces are acting on them to suppress their voices or repress their development? Literature of all types—nursery rhymes, fairy tales, short stories, plays, and novels, as well as the newer storytelling media of television and cinema—clearly delineates how girls are expected to behave. In books for adolescents, it is easy to see how society impinges on girls' choices and behaviors, and the historical novels we explore later in the book are especially effective in pointing this out. For example, upper class New England society in the late 1800s could not tolerate the idea of a female sailor, as demonstrated in *The True Confessions of Charlotte Doyle* (Avi, 1992). In contrast, young girls in the working class of a slightly later era, such as in *Lyddie* (Paterson, 1991), were expected to work long hours in terrible factory conditions without complaint. Both novels illustrate the ways in which young women have been historically constrained to restrictive roles.

Contemporary novels offer the opportunity to explore societal expectations of girls today. *The Wanderer* (Creech, 2000) is a fascinating book to explore in contrast with *The True Confessions of Charlotte Doyle* because it also has as its heroine a young girl who wants to sail. Sadly, it appears that many of the same restrictions against becoming a respected sailor still apply to the modern heroine. However, unlike Charlotte Doyle, *The Wanderer*'s protagonist is able to break free of stereotypes and succeed without abandoning her society.

Fantasy novels are particularly interesting because they create imaginary worlds in which females can be expected to have entirely different functions; however, in many cases they mirror the restrictive societal expectations of the real world. For instance, in *Dragonsong* (McCaffrey, 1976/2003), the heroine longs to be a musician, yet that role is restricted to males in her planet's society.

Using these novels as starting points, the exploration of societal expectations for girls can be extended to the expectations that are in place in the student's own school, community, and nation. The resulting definition of expectations should lead girls to question whether these expectations are realistic and, if not, how they can be resisted. The following questions can help guide discussion on societal influences:

- **What is the role that society expects of the main character in this novel?**
- **Do these expectations match what she believes and values?**
- **What does my society expect of me?**
- **Do I ever act in ways that society expects but that do not match who I am?**

Helping girls to examine how society forms expectations and how girls unknowingly conform can bring about a powerful awakening. Girls often will be amazed at the hidden influences that exist in their schools and in their lives, and how they are affected personally. The next step is to help girls look critically at the roles played by the people around them and to analyze to what extent these people are helping them to resist or hindering them from resisting destructive expectations.

Influence of Adults

Family and peer group are paramount in the life of the adolescent. The way that parental behavior is perceived is especially important to the adolescent because it gives him or her a sense of either security or distress about him- or herself. This in turn gives the adolescent the ability or inability to build successful relationships outside the family.

Parents are obviously the most important figures in girls' development (McHale, Crouter, & Whiteman, 2003). It appears that parental attachment to both mothers and fathers is higher for girls than boys, although it does decline over the teenage years (Buist, Dekovic, Meeus, & van Aken, 2002). Also, there seems to be a somewhat stronger attachment to the parent of the same sex: Boys are more attached to their fathers and girls to their mothers, although this is not always true and can fluctuate during adolescence. Geuzaine, Debry, and Liessens (2000) argue that, although separation from the both parents is necessary, maintaining a connection is very important for girls' successful development as adults. Psychologists today generally reject the idea that there must be a violent break with the parental figure for an adolescent to mature. In fact, a study at Wellesley College showed that girls who felt close to their mothers were more successful in their personal development (Kaplan, Klein, & Gleason, 1991).

Trites (1997) discusses the role of mothers in children's literature in *Waking Sleeping Beauty: Feminist Voices in Children's Novels* and contends that there are very few models of strong mother-daughter relationships in children's literature. According to Trites, most novels adopt one of two types of these relationships: "Those traditional narratives that allow for the daughter to achieve independence from her mother in the classically Oedipal manner...and those less traditional and less Freudian ones that allow the daughter to mature without necessarily breaking from her mother" (p. 103). For instance, *Little Women* (Alcott, 1867/1947) provides a great example of daughters who mature and blossom under the guidance of their wonderfully wise "Marmie;" even the rebellious Jo has a loving relationship with her mother.

Parents are not the only adults who affect the growing adolescent, though. Teachers and coaches also influence the adolescent's perception of his or her strengths and weaknesses. We have already seen how schools too often reveal teachers' expectations of girls to be ones of passivity and compliance. However, many teachers assist girls in their development. Cohen and Blanc (1996), in recommending ways to support girls' development, state,

> Nothing is more important to girls' developing a sense of self than a mentor.... Adults who build relationships with girls over time can help them make sense of their multiple and conflicting roles. Caring adults also bring high expectations. In interviews and focus groups, girls named these adults—almost always women and ranging in position from aide to teacher and principal—as critical to their success. (pp. 86–87)

Coaches also can have positive (or negative) influence on girls, and because of the Title IX enactment, girls are becoming more involved in coached team sports. Often, they have male coaches, which can work for or against them. On one hand, male coaches may demand as high standards of performance from girls as they do for boys; on the other hand, male coaches may expect less from girls because of traditional views of girls' abilities.

Parents, grandparents, coaches, and other adults clearly can influence girls' development of self. They can offer powerful aid by being nurturing and supportive and holding girls to high standards. Caring adults can be role models, listening posts, and counselors to help girls express themselves. However, adult characters in many YA novels do not offer the nurture and support necessary to the young female characters. Reading such novels offers girls a chance to discover how the adults in their lives can affect them.

Parents and Grandparents in Young Adult Literature

In many of the YA novels we analyzed, parents actively suppressed girls' search for their true voices. One of the most shocking examples occurs in the previously mentioned fantasy novel *Dragonsong* (McCaffrey, 1976/2003). The heroine of this novel, Menolly, yearns to be a harper (musician), but in her society women are forbidden to do this. Her parents are so enraged at Menolly's attempt to defy their order to stop playing music that when Menolly's hand is injured, they let the wound heal improperly so Menolly will not be able to play. Another instance of a parent suppressing a daughter is found in the historical novel *Catherine, Called Birdy* (Cushman, 1995): Birdy's father betroths Birdy to a crude, disgusting, elderly (but rich) knight in the hopes of improving the family's fortunes.

It is difficult to find examples of literary mothers and fathers who encourage their daughters to develop their individuality. This is probably not surprising because it is a typical strategy in YA literature to absent the parents, either literally or psychologically, allowing the reader to focus on the young protagonist. Nevertheless, it is a wonderful discussion point that can be used to encourage girls to think about the ways in which their parents affect their development.

Grandparents also play important roles—both positive and negative—in some YA novels. In *The Secret of Gumbo Grove* (Tate, 1987), Raisin Stackhouse's grandmother, Miss Effie, tells Raisin stories about her ancestors. This encourages Raisin to learn about her heritage and question her parents' expectations of her. In contrast, a grandmother has a negative role in *Trouble's Child* (Walter, 1985), which takes place on an isolated island in the Gulf of Mexico. Martha, the granddaughter of the island's wise woman and herbalist, is being pressured to take her grandmother's place, even though Martha wants to leave to study on the mainland. Martha's attempts to please her grandmother interfere with her search for her own voice.

Although family members obviously have the strongest ties and are most likely to affect the adolescent girl, they are not the only adults in girls' lives. Some novels explore the role of other adults in supporting adolescent girls' development.

Teachers, Coaches, and Other Mentors in Young Adult Literature

In some YA novels, teachers, mentors, or coaches encourage the talent and individuality of a young woman. In *Dragonsong* (McCaffrey, 1976/2003) a counterpoint to Menolly's tyrannical father is the Masterharper of Pern, who recognizes Menolly's musical gift and invites her to come study at Harper Hall as an apprentice.

Another example appears in the contemporary novel *Run for Your Life* (Levy, 1996), which tells the story of a group of girls who live in a ghetto and have few opportunities to develop their talents. A young man enters the neighborhood, starts a track team, and encourages the girls to become powerful runners. Kisha, the main character, talks about her coach, Darren:

> He didn't look street, didn't act street. But he wasn't afraid of anyone, or anybody. Not that he shoved people around, or yelled at them, or flexed his muscles—unless he had to. He just had this—presence. This really strong presence. He never said much, but when he talked, after a while, we all sort of listened. I don't know why. Maybe because he believed in us. (pp. 64–65)

In this book, Darren's belief in the girls on the track team causes them to believe in themselves.

It is helpful for girls to learn of the power mentors have in helping them to strengthen their voices. In *Run for Your Life*, it is not only a male coach who helps Kisha and her friends but also an understanding teacher, Ms. Collins, who gives one of the girls a place to stay when it becomes apparent that the girl is being sexually molested by her uncles. Kisha explains,

> Turns out Ms. Collins is okay out of school, too. Just about every day, there she is, standing beside the track when we run. Even when it's cold. She pulls up the collar on her coat, bundles her arms around herself, stamps her feet to keep warm, and cheers us on when we come around to where she's standing. (p. 163)

The positive influences of both the coach and the teacher have a tremendous impact on the development of Kisha's voice and the voice of her friends on the team.

All of these adult figures are interesting to analyze in terms of their influence on the particular book's central character. Girls reading these novels should be able to identify adult figures in their own lives as well as the effect those adults are having on their development and direction. The following questions can direct attention to these issues:

- **Who are the important adults in the main character's life?**
- **What are their expectations of her?**
- **Do these expectations match her beliefs and values?**
- **Who are the important adults in my life?**
- **Do they encourage me to speak out and act on my beliefs and values?**

Influence of Male Peers

As girls enter adolescence, they begin to interact with the males within their peer groups. These males tend to fall into one of three categories—(1) brother, (2) friend, or (3) romantic interest—and often a male who starts out as a friend becomes a romantic interest. Psychological literature concerning the role of brothers in adolescent girls' lives is sparse. There is, however, some interesting information about the roles of friends and boyfriends.

Studies have shown that both boys and girls value friendships with the opposite gender, which become increasingly important during the teenage years. Thomas and Daubman (2001) report that girls especially seem to value friendships with boys. In fact, girls who have male friends report higher self-esteem than those who do not. Nevertheless, girls report that their friendships (with both girls and boys) frequently fail to live up to their expectations. Girls devote a great deal of energy to establishing friendships but often are unable to sustain them. In a successful friendship, girls feel supported and affirmed and are more likely to speak out. This support is especially powerful when it comes from an admired male peer.

Further, the world of the adolescent female is often centered on the quest for a boyfriend. Collins (2003) reports that there has been little serious study of the romantic relationships that occur during adolescence because most psychologists have dismissed these relationships as "trivial and transitory" (p. 1). However, Collins argues that these relationships are more important and involved than previously thought. Collins cites the National Longitudinal Study of Adolescent Health, which reports surveys that indicate that 25% of 12-year-olds describe themselves as having had a serious romantic relationship within the past 18 months. This figure climbs to nearly half of 15-year-olds and 70% of 18-year-olds. In addition, the study suggests that many of these relationships last for 11 months or more.

Teenagers in romantic relationships report increased volatility in mood and feelings of depression. However, Collins (2003) suggests that this may be due to the experience of "breaking up" more than to the relationship itself. In fact, adolescents who are in romantic relationships report higher feelings of self-esteem than those who are not. Again, this may relate to the identity-affirming trait of peer relationships. Being in a relationship enhances the sense of belonging that is so critical to the adolescent. Larson, Wilson, Brown, Furstenberg, and Verma (2002) have postulated that the increasing complexity of today's world may be giving the romantic relationship a more crucial role than it had in the past: that of a buffer against the pressures that are brought to bear on teenagers. According to Collins, there is a great deal about romance that is not understood, either by adults or by teenagers.

Male Friends in Young Adult Literature

How does YA literature portray male peers? Surprisingly, a number of male characters support and nurture the female's quest to establish her own identity, although others clearly fight to suppress it. Several sports books spotlight the various roles that male peers can assume. In *Just for Kicks* (Baczewski, 1990), 15-year-old Brandon convinces his sister, Sarah, to become the kicker for their school's football team. Brandon becomes Sarah's advocate and encourages her to stay with the game. On the other hand, an example of the adversarial role boys can play is found in *There's a Girl in My Hammerlock* (Spinelli, 1993). The central character of the book, eighth-grader Maisie, is good at sports but does not get chosen for the cheerleading squad. In a bid for attention from a star athlete, she tries out for—and is placed on—the wrestling team. The hostility and anger of the boys on her team is matched by the boys on the opposing teams, most of whom refuse to wrestle her.

One of the best examples of a male peer helping a female find her voice is in the contemporary novel *Speak* (Anderson, 2003; see also further discussion in chapter 1). Melinda has been raped at a party and is unable to talk to anyone about it. She retreats to a silent, still world until David, a fellow student, challenges her for refusing to orally report on the suffragette movement:

> But you got it wrong. The suffragettes were all about speaking up, screaming for their rights. You can't speak up for your right to be silent. That's letting the bad guys win. If the suffragettes did that, women wouldn't be able to vote yet. (p. 159)

When Melinda asks, "Do you lecture all your friends like this?" David replies, "Only the ones I like" (p. 159). He is clearly trying to help Melinda express her voice.

Brothers and male friends can be powerful sources of encouragement for adolescent girls; it is helpful for girls to recognize the ones in their lives who are helpful and to seek out male friends who can support them. Boyfriends, on the other hand, can be more problematic, as the quest for romance often leads girls to feel inadequate and insecure.

Boyfriends in Young Adult Literature

Literature often shows the different kinds of romantic attachments that are offered to girls. Two different types are described in *A Ring of Endless Light* (L'Engle, 1981). During the family's annual summer vacation, Adam helps 15-year-old Vicki Austin comes to terms with her grandfather's decline and introduces her to the world of dolphins. He encourages Vicki's interests and supports her emotional growth. Adam contrasts sharply with another suitor, handsome and wealthy Zachary, who tries to mold Vicki into a version of himself, yet is unable to support her through a difficult time. Vicki reflects,

> My excitement about going on a date with Adam was very different from the way I felt when I went out with Zachary. With Zachary I was excited and nervous and somehow playing a role.... With Zachary I wore at least an imaginary costume, because I was trying to live up to his expectations of me, and maybe that was why I felt uncomfortable with him at the same time that I was thrilled. (p. 91)

These two male figures represent clear choices for Vicki: excitement, danger and suppression of her own voice, or reflection, honest discussion, and expression of her true self.

Male-female interaction is critical to young girls entering adolescence. Because girls so desperately seek to be "chosen" for dates, they often lack male friends. When they are not flirting or acting out scripts they have viewed on television, they have difficulty with simple, honest dialogue. (The same is true for boys, of course.) Reading books that explore the concepts of romance and friendship between the sexes may help girls identify more authentic ways of interacting with their male peers. Certainly, discussion of these books will allow girls to see variable ways in which they can relate to adolescent boys, and the following questions may help as well:

- **Who are the important male peers in the main character's life?**
- **What are their expectations of her?**
- **Do these expectations match her beliefs and values?**
- **Who are the important male peers in my life?**
- **Do they encourage me to speak out and act on my beliefs and values?**

Influence of Female Peers

Just as male peers either nurture or reject the adolescent girl's attempt to speak in a true voice, sisters and female peers can assist or subvert a girl's development of voice, too. The whole concept of sisterhood is based on the idea that women support one another. Yet Auerbach (1978) points out in *Communities of Women: An Idea in Fiction* that there have been few communities of women in Western culture. This is in sharp contrast to institutional male communities, such as the military, in which men who fight together develop deep and intricate dependencies upon one another. This idea of male community persists and can be seen in recent popular films such as *Saving Private Ryan* (Segan & Spielberg, 1998), *Black Hawk Down* (Bruckheimer & Scott, 2001), and *Master and Commander: The Far Side of the World* (Goldwyn & Weir, 2003). Although women have now entered the military, they are still largely constrained to noncombatant roles and, therefore, not included in the group's complete network. The close communion of males can also be seen in the concept of team sports, which has only recently been extended to women.

Female Peers in Young Adult Literature

Certainly, in a family, relationships between women are central. Sisters are pivotal characters in many of the books we examined, and in most cases, sisters provide a mixture of support and suppression. Most adolescent girls have conflicted feelings toward their sisters; often they are both admiring and envious of their siblings. Vicki, the protagonist in *A Ring of Endless Light* (L'Engle, 1981) illustrates this struggle beautifully as she thinks about her sister, Suzy:

> I love her. Because she's my sister. I can't imagine the world without her. But I've never talked to her much. I've shared more with Rob than I've ever shared with Suzy. Maybe because Suzy's always been so much better at everything than I have, even little things, like playing catch or spud. Have I been, am I jealous?
>
> Jealous. It's an ugly word. It's an ugly feeling. I don't feel ugly about Suzy. But I don't feel close. So, yes, maybe I am jealous. It's not that I don't want Suzy to have everything she has. But when the gifts were being distributed I'd like to have had a few more. (pp. 253–254)

Frequently this type of sibling rivalry can cause a girl to seek a different persona in an attempt to establish a clear identity. In some cases, this may be helpful.

Other female peers also play a part in whether girls express their authentic voices or try to hide them. In *Dragonsinger* (McCaffrey, 1977/1997), Menolly is selected to attend an academy for harpers (musicians). She is the only female harper at the school, and other girls are spiteful and resentful. Menolly is tempted to play her instrument poorly to lessen their resentment and be accepted as a friend. In the end, however, Menolly has to stand up to them and be herself: an accomplished musician.

Female friends can bolster a girl's attempt to find her true voice; however, most of the books we reviewed did not illustrate this type of friendship. This can make for interesting discussion as female students reflect on how their female peers affect their attempts to acquire a voice:

- **Who are the important female peers in my life?**
- **What are their expectations of me?**
- **Do these expectations match my beliefs and values?**
- **Do they encourage me to speak out and act on my beliefs and values?**

Influence of Physical Appearance

Ask teenage girls what the most important asset they could have to be successful is, and most will say "looking good" or "being pretty." In one 1998 study, over half of the young women between ages 12 and 15 who were surveyed listed appearance as the biggest concern in their lives (Anorexia Nervosa and Related Eating Disorders, Inc., n.d.). Lookism, a term coined in 1978, is defined as prejudice against those who do not meet standards of physical beauty (Safire, 2000).

Beauty has been a trademark of the female gender in Western society since the times of the ancient Greeks and Romans. Fairy tales such as "Sleeping Beauty" and "Beauty and the Beast" actually name the female character with the trait. Of course, female beauty is primarily important in attracting men. Helen of Troy is perhaps the most classic example; Paris was so attracted to Helen that he stole her from her husband, thus causing the launch of "a thousand ships" and a war that toppled a healthy society.

It is worth noting that extreme beauty often seems to exact a price, which in some cases is the result of jealousy and retribution from other females. For instance, the queen's question to the mirror in Snow White—"Mirror, mirror on the wall/Who's the fairest of them all?"—results in an unwelcome answer that leads to attempted murder. The queen is willing to poison Snow White to capture the title of "fairest of them all." Generally, however, beauty is rewarded in Western mythology by the adoration of men and a path to high status, such as marriage to a prince. As chapter 1 of this book points out, popular culture today suggests to adolescent girls that they should do anything to attain and keep physical beauty.

The Changing Face of Beauty

The definition of beauty changes all the time. Even in the last 100 years, there has been a dramatic revision of what it means to be beautiful. *The Body Project: An Intimate History of American Girls* (Brumberg, 1998) describes the changes in what is perceived as beautiful in women in the United States. In the 1920s, it became fashionable to be very thin; women bound their breasts to look boyish and slender. By the 1950s, curvy, voluptuous figures were in vogue— Marilyn Monroe was the ideal. In the 1960s, boyish figures once again became popular, as demonstrated by models such as Twiggy, and thinness has held sway since that time. Hairstyles have always varied widely, from the "bob" of the 1920s and the perms and curls of the 1940s and 1950s to hair that was ironed straight in the 1960s and the "big hair" of the 1970s. Perfect skin has consistently been sought, and acne and blemishes often cause hysteria among young women. Since the 1990s, however, the trends of tattooing and piercing that perfect skin have emerged. Brumberg summarizes the changes that have occurred regarding physical beauty:

> Although girls in the past and present display many common developmental characteristics—such as self-consciousness, sensitivity to peers, and an interest in establishing an independent identity— before the twentieth century, girls simply did not organize their thinking about themselves around their bodies. Today, many young girls worry about the contours of their bodies—especially shape, size, and muscle tone—because they believe that the body is the ultimate expression of the self. (p. 97)

The focus on female beauty has provided a myriad of opportunities for commercial exploitation. Literally hundreds of companies exist that provide cosmetics to enhance skin, hair, and nails. Clothing and shoe stores for women employ thousands; one of the most wildly successful enterprises in recent years, Victoria's Secret, sells primarily lingerie (and is marketing it to younger and younger women). Women are spending inordinate amounts of money to look better. A relatively new trend is the extensive use of plastic surgery to reshape both face and body. Once restricted to wealthy older clients, the practice is now utilized by young women who undergo cosmetic surgery with the help of long-term payment plans. Thus the selling of beauty has intensified the already severe pressure on girls to look good.

Some of the casualties in the war for beauty are the number of girls who starve themselves in the hope of becoming thinner and thus more attractive. As girls enter adolescence, their bodies begin to produce fat for the storage of estrogen. This very normal development that takes place during adolescence results in a disconnect between the media picture of the perfect teenager and what some girls see in the mirror, causing them to experience intense dissatisfaction with their bodies (Striegel-Moore & Cachelin, 1999). This dissatisfaction may lead to dieting and even more drastic measures such as fasting or purging. It is estimated that between 1% and 3% of girls develop either anorexia or bulimia as a result of these practices. Both of those diseases are potentially life threatening and difficult to treat. There are a large number of other girls who exhibit disordered eating habits that they carry with them to adulthood, perhaps contributing to other health problems. Even more troubling, this concern with body weight appears to be affecting girls of younger and younger ages. Girls as young as age five have expressed the desire to be thinner, and it is common to hear second graders discussing dieting ("Body obsession," 2001).

What role do perceived physical beauty and lookism play in how girls develop their voices? Media messages combine to prescribe to girls the look they must have to be acceptable. Thus, often the idea of looking like themselves is unacceptable; they need to look like Britney Spears or Beyoncé or whoever is the poster girl of the year. Conformity on the outside is the first step to conformity on the inside. In other words, a girl who is willing to go to extremes to change her physical appearance most likely will suppress her authentic voice as well.

Physical Appearance and Lookism in Young Adult Literature

Because the connection between womanhood and physical beauty is so strong, it is impossible to read literature about adolescent girls that does not address the issue of appearance. The majority of books written for teenage girls foster the assumption that girls will do anything in their power to enhance their attractiveness. Some books contest this assumption, although these books are still too rare. Some force readers to confront physical deformity; others try to reveal the masking effect of beauty aids such as cosmetics and clothing. It is worth looking for these books because they challenge girls to think deeply about what they want their voices to be.

One of the most powerful novels to suggest that girls challenge the quest for physical perfection is *Izzy, Willy-Nilly* (Voigt, 1995). At the beginning of the book, Izzy (short for Isabelle) is an attractive, popular cheerleader. Tragically, a car accident causes her to lose part of a leg. She can no longer be a cheerleader. Even worse, she is shunned by all of her former friends because they cannot bear to be around a person who is physically damaged. Much of the book centers on Izzy coming to terms with her physical impairment. Izzy finally realizes her worth as a person has to do with who she is, not what she looks like, and her increasing awareness of her own self-worth makes her a more interesting character.

The use of makeup is often a metaphor for the creation of a mask that hides individuality and makes girls conform to a certain look. In *The Golden Compass* (Pullman, 2001), young Lyra is bewitched by the enchanting Mrs. Coulter, who brings her to live in the city and attempts to mold her into a duplicate of herself:

> And finally, there were other kinds of lessons so gently and subtly given that they didn't feel like lessons at all. How to wash one's own hair; how to judge which colors suited one; how to say no in such a charming way that no offense was given; how to put on lipstick, powder, scent. To be sure, Mrs. Coulter didn't teach Lyra the latter arts directly, but she knew Lyra was watching when she made herself up, and she took care to let Lyra see where she kept the cosmetics, and to allow her time on her own to explore and try them out for herself. (p. 83)

The makeup is symbolic of Mrs. Coulter's attempts to impose a false persona on Lyra. Fortunately, Lyra rejects the imposition.

One of the most dramatic books to explore the effects of lookism is *Staying Fat for Sarah Byrnes* (Crutcher, 2003). Sarah is a high school girl whose face has been badly burned in a kitchen accident. Her father has refused to let her receive surgery to repair her scars, so her face is a hideous mask. As a result, Sarah is ostracized by all of her high school contemporaries except one, the narrator of the novel. In one of the highlights of the book, Sarah says to her loyal friend "...look at me, Eric. Look at me! I'm never going to be okay! Never!" Eric replies, "No, Sarah Byrnes, you're wrong. You're just never going to be pretty.... But you are going to be okay" (p. 159). The distinction between looks and substance is key to the novel—and key to any meaningful discussion of this topic.

If girls are to be encouraged to find their true voices, then they must be made aware of the intense pressure placed on women through thousands of years of history, now magnified by the media and commercial interests, that urges them to conform to specific looks. This pressure cannot be overstated, as it can result in such dire conditions as eating disorders and depression (see chapter 3 for further discussion these topics). The following questions can be used to focus students on the effects of the quest for perfect appearance and lookism:

- **What are the physical looks that are valued in this novel?**
- **In what ways does the main character try to conform to this look, if at all?**
- **What are looks that are valued in my school, community, and culture?**
- **To what degree do my looks match this description?**
- **What is the look that best expresses my self, what I believe and value?**

Influence of Physical and Emotional Changes of Adolescence

The years from ages 10 through 16 are incredibly turbulent; as children enter adolescence, they experience many physical and emotional changes. For instance, girls begin to menstruate, a process that initiates the production of estrogen and progesterone. These hormones affect the hypothalamus, which in turn affects the pituitary gland (Gray & Phillips, 1998). Each month, girls experience symptoms that may include nausea, bloating, cramps, and pain. Young women find themselves crying for no apparent reason, experience broad mood swings, and even sometimes have suicidal thoughts. If they are fortunate, they have mothers or older sisters who teach them about what is happening to their bodies. The middle and high school curricula for some states require health classes that include this information ("Health framework for California," 2003; "Health education standards of learning for Virginia," 2001). However, the opportunity is limited for students to discuss the personal and psychological impacts that the changes they are undergoing have on their own lives.

Portrayal of Physical and Emotional Changes in Young Adult Literature

What is the impact of these rapid body changes or lack of them? One of the most engaging novels that explores this topic is *Are You There, God? It's Me, Margaret* (Blume, 1972). Sixth-grade student Margaret has many questions for God, including when she is going to fill out her training bra. Margaret is also terribly afraid that she will be the last girl in her peer group to get her period. She prays,

> Are you there God? It's me, Margaret. Gretchen, my friend, got her period. I'm so jealous God. I hate myself for being so jealous, but I am. I wish you'd help me just a little. Nancy's sure she's going to get it soon, too. And if I'm last I don't know what I'll do. Oh please God, I just want to be normal. (p. 100)

This light-hearted yet insightful book encourages girls to explore the physical changes they experience at the onset of adolescence and to consider what these changes mean.

Another wonderful novel that explores girls' physical changes is *Come a Stranger* (Voigt, 1986). At the beginning of the book, Mina, an African American child, is chosen to attend a summer camp for gifted ballerinas. The next year, her main focus becomes returning to the camp. However, by the next summer her body has changed, and she is no longer a promising ballerina; sadly, she is asked to leave the camp. She begs to be allowed to stay, but her request is refused and she is told to admit that she has failed. Voigt writes,

> At that, Mina was so angry that she did burst into tears. She was so angry she just wept. She was weeping so hard she couldn't speak. Just growing wasn't failure, you couldn't say someone had failed just

because her body grew bosoms and hips and the muscles worked differently. (p. 76)

Mina's struggle to accept her changed body and to find a new path is the crux of the story. Fortunately, she is able to find a new direction for her life.

It is disappointing that few of the books we have read deal in depth with the normal physical and emotional changes of adolescence. We know, however, that these issues are important sources of discussion, so we hope more books in the future will address these critical parts of the adolescent experience. Questions that can help girls address these issues are as follows:

- **What physical and emotional changes are experienced by the main character in this novel? Are her peers going through the same things, or does she feel alone in her experiences?**
- **How does the character deal with these changes?**
- **What physical and emotional changes am I experiencing?**
- **How are these changes affecting me and my understanding of myself?**

Introducing Students to Forces That Suppress or Encourage Voice

There are several ways to introduce students to the forces that encourage or suppress the voice of the adolescent girl before tackling a study of one of the novels. Probably the simplest way is to use a well-known fairy tale. For example, in the fairy tale Cinderella, the influences of adults, peers, and especially lookism can be clearly identified. Taking each element of the organizing frame seen in Figure 1 (see page 23), students can discuss the questions illustrated in Figure 2.

There are excellent novels that use fairy tales as a basis but transform the girls into more interesting characters; for example, both *Just Ella* (Haddix, 2001) and *Ella Enchanted* (Levine, 1998) explore the story of Cinderella from a more modern perspective. It would be highly instructive for students to read one of these novels after a discussion of the traditional Cinderella story and then compare and contrast the answers each tale provides to the questions in Figure 2.

Another helpful way to introduce students to the concepts of the varying roles of their peers, lookism, and the developmental changes that occur during adolescence is to use a modern story that probably has been read (or viewed) by most of the students. For example, the character Hermione Granger, of *Harry Potter* fame (e.g., Rowling, 1998), is an interesting study. The framework discussion guide would look like Figure 3.

In all likelihood, the questions asked will elicit heated discussion. Some students will argue that Hermione is focused on becoming a wizard, but others may contend that she is too cautious and unwilling to break the rules, or that she too eagerly tries to be the "teacher's

Figure 2   Using the Expression/Suppression Framework to Discuss Cinderella

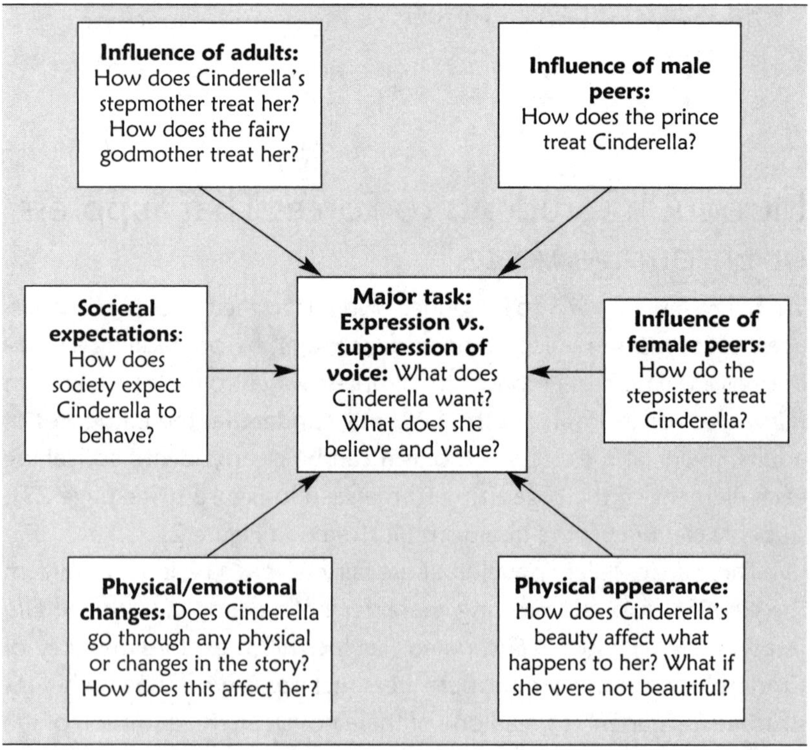

Influence of adults:
How does Cinderella's stepmother treat her? How does the fairy godmother treat her?

Influence of male peers:
How does the prince treat Cinderella?

Societal expectations:
How does society expect Cinderella to behave?

Major task: Expression vs. suppression of voice: What does Cinderella want? What does she believe and value?

Influence of female peers:
How do the stepsisters treat Cinderella?

Physical/emotional changes: Does Cinderella go through any physical or changes in the story? How does this affect her?

Physical appearance:
How does Cinderella's beauty affect what happens to her? What if she were not beautiful?

pet." Her male peers, in the forms of Harry Potter and Ron Weasley, are instrumental in encouraging Hermione to take more risks and learn more about wizardry. They also get her into trouble. Is that good or bad? The influence of other girls is curiously absent in Hermione's world, and students may wish to discuss why this is so. In the wizarding world, females clearly are expected to perform heroic tasks and to master the art of wizardry; yet in both Harry Potter's nonwizard family and in the wizard Weasley family, the wives seem to fulfill a traditional role (i.e., not working, supporting their husbands, cooking, cleaning, and so on). Will Hermione eventually fall into this role? Almost any book (or movie) with a strong female figure can be discussed using this lens.

Figure 3 Using the Expression/Suppression Framework to Discuss the Character Hermione in the Harry Potter Books

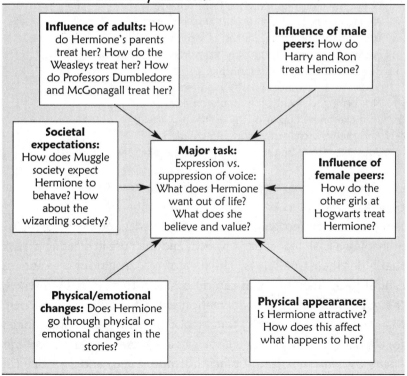

A third way to introduce students to the ideas embedded in the framework is through poetry. A wonderful collection of poetry by girls is found in *I Wouldn't Thank You for a Valentine: Poems for Young Feminists* (Duffy, 1997). Some of these poems speak directly to various issues that affect adolescent girls, for example, "Self-Portraits" by Elma Mitchell (Duffy, 1997):

The cupboard contains my dresses, the drawer my faces.

Seven selves lie on seven shelves.
I try them on every night, a concoction of fig-leaves
To cover all possible cases. I am Juliet,
Cleopatra, Marilyn—everyone, except naked
Susanna Smith, my mother and father's daughter.
I owe nobody the make of my body.
I bought myself at Boots—the cosmetic counter
And the slimming aids. I shopped for myself in windows
And women's magazines, and then in the long, long mirrors
In the eyes of the watchers of birds.
I twist my mouth in the glass. I peer anxiously,
And erase, and alter—the artist after perfection
With pencil and brush, the ladies' do-it-yourself
Portable Rembrandt, the only self-portrait that has to
Be painted afresh every morning.
      Nice work, in its way—
Not boring, certainly, the supple capacity
To make oneself up as one goes, to carry the light
And rainbow style of continuous creation
But I like myself best in the bath, where it all comes off. (p. 41)

This poem speaks clearly to the issue of how society's portrayal of perfect beauty works to suppress a girl's authentic self. Girls will certainly be able to recognize the role of cosmetics and "slimming aids" in shaping a look that society expects, and their use in creating a mask that hides their true selves. The idea of a "continuous creation" is central to the idea that girls can choose how to portray themselves; the question is whether that creation will reflect the authentic self. Many other books of poetry for girls also offer excellent opportunities for analysis; two interesting anthologies are *These Are Not Sweet Girls: Poetry by Latin American Women* (Allende, 2000) and *Girls Like Us:*

40 Extraordinary Women Celebrate Girlhood in Story, Poetry, and Song (Misiroglu, 1999).

Summary

The purpose of this chapter has been to explore the various forces at work in causing girls to express or to suppress their voices. Using literature as a lens, girls can engage in discussions about protagonists (and other female characters) who are being pressured to conform to societal expectations but who are able to resist those pressures. Adults (such as parents, teachers, coaches, and other role models) and peers (including boyfriends, girlfriends, and siblings) should be scrutinized for their part in encouraging or silencing the characters' voices. Special attention should be paid to the pressure to look pretty. Introductory lessons can be taught using poetry, film, or familiar fairy tales as stories for analysis. Depending on the setting of the book discussion, all of these vehicles might be used to introduce students to key contributors to or inhibitors of voice before reading a novel. The more students recognize and understand the forces that act upon adolescent girls, the more insight they will bring to discussions of the books they read. The next chapters outline specific genres and books that can provide rich opportunities for teachers and their students to explore female characters.

CHAPTER 3

Contemporary Realistic Fiction, Contemporary Issues

Kyle Lumsden teaches ninth-grade English. He knows that the girls in his classes are generally quieter and less likely to speak out in classroom discussion than are the boys in his class, although some of his African American girls are very vocal. Because Kyle himself is young, he is struck by the idea of using literature to help his students find their voices. Kyle is intrigued by asking students these simple questions: Who am I? What do I believe? What do I value? He realizes that he is still asking those questions of himself.

Kyle is committed to teaching with young adult (YA) literature. He has already set a policy in his classroom by which students are required to independently read one novel a month. His students are average, so he tries to pick novels that are relatively short and easy to read. Most of the students do read the assigned novel, so Kyle sets aside one Friday a month for discussion and writing about it. Kyle has implemented a format that works: first, discussion about the book; second, some kind of personal, private writing; and third, some type of public writing assignment that will be shared. The school uses a block-schedule format, so Kyle has about 75 minutes to use for this purpose.

Kyle wants to find a book that focuses on the expression of voice versus suppression of it. He is interested in one that shows the struggle that girls have but because of his gender hopes to find one that also includes a male perspective. He begins to look through his library. Because of his interest in today's pressures, he restricts his search to contemporary YA novels that contain issues with which his female students struggle. The high school counselor spoke to the staff recently about how many students are believed to be using alcohol and drugs on a regular basis. Teen pregnancy is another real concern at his school—Kyle has one student in his third-period class who has already had a baby, and several others whose teenage sisters have at least one child. He is also concerned about a few girls in his class who seem exceptionally thin—one is almost skeletal. Kyle is aware that several of his students, both boys and girls, are on prescription antidepressant medication. There was a suicide in the school last year, and the memory haunts the staff. Kyle wonders if he should pick a book that addresses one of these pressures.

KYLE'S CONCERNS and teaching ideas are right on target. As we consider the genres of YA literature that most readily address the issues faced by girls today, it becomes apparent that realistic fiction offers the most direct approach. Works of contemporary realistic fiction are written with the purpose of connecting to their young readers by offering settings and events that are comparable to the ones that tweens and teens experience in the course of their daily lives.

Expression vs. Suppression: The Quest for Voice in Contemporary Realistic Fiction

In the contemporary YA novel, there are clear distinctions between girls who express their authentic selves and those who desperately seek conformity within today's social precepts. Many of the books that girls love show them how they can become popular. But a wonderful example of expressing one's uniqueness can be found in *Stargirl* (Spinelli, 2002). The story of Stargirl (whose birth name is Susan Carroway) is told from the point of view of Leo, a high school junior in a school where

> ...we all wore the same clothes, talked the same way, ate the same food, listened to the same music. Even our dorks and nerds had a MAHS stamp on them. If we happened to somehow distinguish ourselves, we quickly snapped back into place like rubber bands. (p. 10)

Then tenth-grade Stargirl arrives, coming from nine years of home schooling. Stargirl wears costumes to school: one day a prairie dress, another a flapper outfit, another a kimono. She decorates each desk that she sits in. She has a pet rat, Cinnamon, that she brings to school. She brings her ukulele and serenades different students in the lunchroom. At first Stargirl is adored as a novelty, but gradually she becomes a pariah. The other students shun her and pretend she is not there. Meanwhile, Leo has fallen in love with Stargirl, and they start spending time together; he begs Stargirl to be like the other girls at school because he cannot handle being shunned by other students. Stargirl tries to become Susan, but she is miserable and so returns to her eccentric behavior. Leo breaks up with her, but much later he realizes what he has lost.

Stargirl is a terrific book to use to illustrate the idea of expressing one's authentic self. It shows how difficult it is for a teenage girl to be different and what a high price is sometimes demanded of her if she does not conform. But when we use this book in our college class, the written reflections of our students always include many comments that relay a similar message: "I wish I were more like Stargirl."

Aside from examining the central issue of how to be true to oneself, contemporary realistic YA novels address other difficult issues that young people experience. Beginning with the publication of S.E. Hinton's *The Outsiders* (1967/2003), teen novels began to deal with subjects such as violence, bullying, prejudice against class and ethnicity, pregnancy, and other previously taboo topics. Interestingly, the author of *The Outsiders* was a 16-year-old girl, and she has said that she wanted to write about the things that she saw happening at her high school, which included gang fights, bullying and intimidation, murder, and self-sacrifice. Since that time, novels have tackled many other difficult subjects: drug abuse, homosexuality, rape, and incest, to name only a few. These texts deservedly are labeled "problem novels." According to Nilsen and Donelson (2001), the problem novel departs from the idea that young people's fiction should provide examples of uplifting experiences and good role models. Problem novels are "based on a different philosophy. The idea is that young people have a better chance to be happy if they have realistic expectations and if they know both the bad and the good about the society in which they live" (Nilsen & Donelson, 2001, p. 115). What follows is discussion of some of the major issues we feel girls should explore in their reading, as well as suggestions for quality novels teachers can use to open this important dialogue.

Drug and Alcohol Abuse

According to Esman (1990), drug use in the United States prior to World War II was exclusively restricted to those outside the mainstream, often musicians. But in the 1970s the use of marijuana became a "rite of passage for middle class adolescents; for some it became and remained a significant part of their lives, although for most it came to occupy a less central, largely recreational role" (p. 56). In the 1980s and 1990s, cocaine began to replace marijuana as the drug of choice, but the development of "crack" cocaine, a highly addictive form of the drug, introduced a far more serious element to adolescent drug use. Cocaine is much more expensive than marijuana, which can be easily grown in the United States, and cocaine's cost plus its addictive properties made criminal control of its sale and distribution inevitable.

It is generally assumed that drug use is a sign of teenage rebellion, a way of defying authority. However, studies have shown that most teen drug users "conform in many ways with conventional values, including a strong work ethic and an aspiration toward bourgeois standards of social achievement" (Esman, 1990, p. 60). Pipher (1994) suggests that teens use drugs to seek thrills or altered states of consciousness. Esman postulates that drug use and even criminal activity represent a way for some teens to achieve status "in a world that offers them little opportunity to do so through 'legitimate' channels" (p. 60).

Esman and Pipher both point out that the most typical drug chosen by adolescents is alcohol. It is cheap and readily accessible. According to Thomas (2002), an analysis of national data conducted by the National Center on Addiction and Substance Abuse in 1999 found that alcohol use among teenagers was reported by 48% of girls and 52% of boys. Binge drinking, which means drinking five or more drinks at a time, was reported by 31% of girls and 34% of boys. This represents a major shift in the data, which previously showed far more alcohol use by boys. Pipher emphasizes that drug and alcohol use is often symptomatic of other problems as well, which leads us to believe that our hypothesis is correct: Girls face increasing pressures nowadays—and have few positive outlets.

Drug and Alcohol Abuse in Young Adult Literature

Two YA novels that deal with drug abuse during different time periods are *Go Ask Alice* (Anonymous, 1967/1998) and *Smack* (Burgess, 1999). *Go Ask Alice* purports to be the diary of a teenage girl who is lonely and awkward. At the beginning of the book, 14-year-old Alice is ditched by the boy she loves and sinks into a deep depression. When her family moves so her father can take a new job, Alice is thrilled. Unfortunately, the move isolates her and makes her desperate to fit in. At a party, one of her friends spikes her drink with LSD, and she experiences exhilarating highs. She begins to use drugs, at first recreationally, then habitually. When she realizes that she has become an addict, she stops using drugs and endures the tortures of withdrawal. It appears that Alice has been rescued from her addiction. But at the very end of the novel, the reader learns to his or her horror that she has begun to use drugs again and is unable to live without them.

When the book was first published, it was assumed to be an actual diary: Many teens still believe it is an authentic first-person narrative, although it is not. The author wrote it as a cautionary tale about the negative effects of drugs. Although the book has received little attention for its literary merit, it is still beloved by many teen readers and is often read aloud in schools because of its unwavering antidrug message. The book illustrates the strong connection between drug use and lack of self-esteem: Alice turns to drugs to ameliorate her sense of despair and disconnection because she has so little sense of her own worth.

Smack is a modern tale of drug abuse. Although it is in many ways more terrifying than *Go Ask Alice*, it does offer a degree of hope. Burgess based this story on actual people, which makes it chillingly realistic. The story is told by multiple first-person narrators who live in the town of Bristol, England. Sixteen-year-old Tar and 14-year-old

Gemma decide to run away from their restrictive (and in Tar's case, alcoholic and abusive) parents. They meet other runaways who are squatting in vacant buildings. A slightly older couple, Lily and Rob, take the teens in and introduce them to the lifestyle of the young and homeless—a lifestyle that includes the use of heroin. Gradually, Tar and Gemma become as dependent on the drug as Lily and Rob already are. After they use up all of Gemma's money, they resort to prostitution and theft to feed their habit. At first none of the four admits that he or she is addicted, but when Lily becomes pregnant she decides to quit, and her three friends agree to join her. They go to the country and there try to deal with their withdrawals, but they cannot tolerate them and end up desperately trying to get drugs. Lily returns to heroin use, at one point nursing her baby while at the same time trying to find a vein in her chest into which to inject heroin.

The tone of the novel is nonjudgmental, allowing the horror of the teens' descent into drug use to drive the story. Although the characters are British, U.S. teenagers have responded strongly to the novel's graphic depictions. Girls in particular identify with Gemma, who runs away from a fairly normal home and must deal with the consequences of a different reality. Gemma's fate, although it involves pregnancy and early motherhood, is somewhat hopeful compared to Alice's. Girls can consider why Gemma is able to overcome her drug addiction, while Alice cannot. The following questions can help teachers lead further classroom discussion on novels about teen drug and alcohol abuse:

- Why does the main character (or characters) begin using drugs?
- What peer pressure or societal forces are influences?
- Who or what causes the characters to continue or stop using drugs? How?
- What would you do if you had a friend who began using drugs?
- How do family relationships play a role in whether someone uses drugs? What conversations have you had with parents or other adults about drugs?

- How does the crowd with which someone hangs out affect whether he or she might try drugs and/or become a regular user?
- What opportunities arise for the character(s) to get help with drug addiction or alcohol abuse? What help is available for people in real life who use drugs or abuse alcohol?
- What could you tell a younger sibling or friend about drugs and alcohol to caution them against these dangers?

Depression and Suicide

One of the major dangers of teenage life is depression. Koplewicz (2002), in his excellent book *More Than Moody: Recognizing and Treating Adolescent Depression*, points out that even in 1989 the Journal of the American Medical Association reported that "depression seems to be occurring earlier in life than ever before" (p. 14). Women are particularly susceptible to depression. According to Koplewicz, studies suggest than 1 of every 5 women (as opposed to 1 of every 10 men) will develop depression at some point in her life. This holds true for adolescent girls as well. Koplewicz reports the warning signs of teenage depression, taken from the National Institute of Mental Health:

- Persistently sad or irritable mood
- Loss of interest in activities once enjoyed
- Significant change in sleeping patterns or appetite
- Loss of energy
- Feelings of worthlessness or inappropriate guilt
- Difficulty concentrating
- Recurrent thoughts of suicide
- Frequent vague, unspecific physical complaints
- Frequent absences from school, cutting classes, drop in academic performance
- Outbursts of shouting, complaining, irritability, crying; increased anger/hostility

- Excessive boredom
- Social isolation
- Alcohol or drug abuse
- Fear of death
- Extreme sensitivity to rejection or failure
- Reckless behavior (pp. 20–21)

According to Koplewicz (2002), the risk of depression peaks at ages 13 and 14. There are many factors that predispose adolescents to depression, including genetic markers and excessive stress brought on by events such as death or divorce in the family. However, Koplewicz notes that adolescence is almost always stressful, so many adolescents are at risk.

Melinda, the main character in *Speak* (Anderson, 2003; described in further detail in chapter 1) exhibits classic symptoms of depression after being raped at a high school party. She withdraws from life and communication with others. Another novel that addresses depression is *Izzy, Willy-Nilly* (Voigt, 1995; discussed in chapter 2). Izzy, a high school cheerleader, is invited to a party with a popular senior. At the party, Marco, her date, drinks too much and Izzy is afraid to go home with him. Against her better judgement, she does, and they are involved in a serious accident. Izzy's legs are damaged and one has to be amputated. Izzy is ousted from the popular crowd, and she becomes deeply depressed. She reflects:

> I could see why they thought I was adjusting so well. But I knew I wasn't. It was as if my life had cracked in half, and the two parts of it were as different as night and day. The day Izzy was the one everybody saw and talked to. The night Izzy, only I knew about. She was scared; she did a lot of weeping and whining alone in her room. She was ashamed of herself, and she tried hard to make herself accept what had happened, but she couldn't accept it. I couldn't accept it. (p. 209)

Finally, Izzy finds a new friend, Rosamunde, who is unconventional but able to deal with reality. Over time and with Rosamunde's help, Izzy is able to accept her new body and face the world.

Both of these books provide examples of depression caused by traumatic events. However, many teenagers become depressed without these triggers, which makes it more difficult for others to understand why they are in despair. At its worst, this despair can also lead to suicide. *Night Falls Fast: Understanding Suicide* (Jamison, 1999) gives a comprehensive look at the causes and effects of suicide. Of particular concern is the rate of suicide among young people. Jamison cites a 1997 Youth Risk Behavior study that surveyed over 16,000 high school students. Of those questioned, 20% (one of every five) said that they had seriously considered suicide; 16% had an actual plan that described in detail how they were going to kill themselves. This study has been replicated with similar and even more distressing findings: One study found that 50% of New York high school students had had thoughts of suicide (Jamison, 1999, p. 47). Fortunately, most suicidal thoughts do not result in action, but Jamison reports that the rate of suicide of children ages 10 to 14 increased by 120% between 1980 and 1992. She states, "In 1995, more teenagers and young adults died from suicide than died from cancer, heart disease, AIDS, pneumonia, influenza, birth defects and stroke combined" (p. 48). Jamison posits many reasons why the suicide rate for young people may be climbing, including effective psychiatric medicines that allow people with emotional illnesses to marry and have children at risk for psychiatric disorders; smoking and drug use during pregnancy, which can result in babies with low birth weights and behavioral disorders; and the decreasing age of the onset of puberty, upon which she places the most significance.

Depression and Suicide in Young Adult Literature

The Turning Hour (Mickle, 2001), explores the topic of attempted suicide. In this contemporary YA novel, beautiful, talented high school senior Bergin decides to end her life by overdosing on aspirin. Her stepbrother returns home early and finds her, saving her life. Bergin, however, does not wish to live. The book is told in the alternating voices of Bergin and her mother, Leslie, who feels responsible for Bergin's suicide attempt and is determined to identify its cause. Fortunately, both Leslie and Bergin are helped by a remarkable psychiatrist who is able to lead them to important discoveries about themselves and their pasts. By the end of the book, Bergin becomes aware of the precious gift of life and realizes that she does not want to squander it.

This novel is extremely effective in showing that suicide can happen even in apparently functional families and to seemingly intact young people. It provides an example of the powerful help that is available to young people in crisis. Fortunately, Bergin has many people who love her and are determined to help her get well, particularly her mother. Because her mother was emotionally damaged herself as a young girl, she also undergoes a painful examination of her feelings and actions to help Bergin. Young people who are not surrounded by such love and support might not be able to navigate through their pain so easily, however. The focus of *The Turning Hour* is more on the healing process than the actual suicide attempt, and there is no repeat of attempted self-injury.

Mickle has discussed her reasons for writing a book about teen suicide. A woman approached her at the beach because she had read two of Mickle's previous novels. She told Mickle that her daughter, a high school senior, had tried to commit suicide and that the subsequent healing process had actually enriched the whole family. Mickle was initially reluctant to tackle this taboo subject and finally called a friend who was a psychologist. The friend said, "My God, Shelley, you've got to do it. You won't believe how many young men and women I see in my practice each month who have attempted to end their lives" ("Author Profile: Shelley Fraser Mickle," 2002, para. 6). In Mickle's research of adolescent suicide, she found out that 40% of teens who attempt suicide drop out of follow-up psychological treatment. This fact, among others, convinced her to write *The Turning Hour*. She states, "I think a novel such as *The Turning Hour* may be able to reach young adults in ways that conventional treatment cannot—and aid in prevention" (para. 10).

The following questions may help open classroom discussion about depression and suicide:

• Why do Izzy and Bergin fall into depression? How do their family and friends react?

- How do Izzy and Bergin see themselves differently during their depression?
- What friends or family members help the character overcome depression? How?
- Are Izzy and Bergin stronger people after they overcome their depression? How?
- What would you do if you had a friend who you suspected was depressed?

Self-Mutilation

Although most girls do not attempt suicide, there is a distressing trend developing where they do harm themselves physically in other ways. School psychologist Richard Lieberman (2004) characterizes self-mutilation as "one of the least understood behaviors of adolescence" that "appears to be increasing at a staggering rate" (p. 10). Lieberman explains that the most common type of self-mutilation includes repeated patterns of cutting, burning, picking at wounds, head banging, and other self-destructive behaviors, with cutting being the most prevalent.

Studies suggest that few young people who engage in cutting or other self-destructive behaviors are actually trying to commit suicide (Lieberman, 2004; Muehlenkamp & Gutierrez, 2004). On the contrary, they are trying to relieve their emotional pain and feel better, although in a maladaptive way. Self-mutilation usually is done episodically, often triggered by an emotional event, and it is gratifying and thus addictive. The behavior is believed to trigger natural antidepressants in the brain, which makes the subject feel better, at least temporarily. However, its aftereffects often include feelings of guilt and shame. Although Muehlenkamp and Gutierrez (2004) report that estimates of teens who engage in self-injurious behavior range from 5.1% to over 40% of all adolescents, Lieberman (2004) reports that in middle and high school approximately 80% of teens who mutilate themselves are female.

Self-Mutilation in Young Adult Literature

There are not many books that tackle cutting behavior, and Lieberman (2004) cautions that this behavior can be "contagious" and videos or group discussions of the subject can trigger more incidents. Two novels, however, have received high praise from teen readers and are worth careful classroom discussion: *The Luckiest Girl in the World* (Levenkron, 1998) and *Cut* (McCormick, 2000).

The protagonist of *The Luckiest Girl in the World*, Katie Roskova, is an ice skater. Her mother is fixated on the idea that Katie will be an Olympic contender. She has devoted her life to making sure that Katie has intensive skating lessons and private coaching. Her obsession with her daughter's success has driven away Katie's father. Katie tries desperately to please her mother and to achieve her dreams, but she simply lacks the savagely competitive drive that her mother has. On the outside Katie is beautiful and confident, but inside she is in despair. This inner conflict leads Katie to start cutting herself. After she has a complete breakdown in front of the entire school, her cutting behavior is discovered and she is forced to attend weekly therapy sessions. Through these sessions, she confronts the abuse that her mother has subjected her to and begins to regain her emotional health.

The Luckiest Girl in the World graphically illustrates the effect of cutting on Katie's ability to function. It clearly describes the behavior as a way of handling psychological problems:

> The wound she made was really only a nick, but the pain she inflicted on herself steadied her. The wild, out-of-control feeling started to go away. The pain was doing its work. She repeated the movement again. This time the cut was longer and deeper. Blood came to the surface. The sight of the red drops on her skin calmed her even more. Her heart returned to its normal rhythm; she could breathe again. The blood held her gaze, the pain made her mind focus and kept it centered in her body. She knew she wasn't going to space out now. Relief flooded through her. (p. 20)

Callie, the protagonist of *Cut*, has been admitted to a psychiatric residential facility because of her cutting behavior. Her parents are at a loss, and Callie does not seem to know why she is cutting herself. The book reveals Callie's motives through group therapy sessions, conversations with the other girls at the facility, and individual sessions with a caring doctor. Gradually, Callie begins to understand the incredible stress she lives under, which is caused by an ill younger brother, a depressed mother, and a distant father. She finds a way to get help, and she commits herself to stopping her destructive behavior.

Both *The Luckiest Girl in the World* and *Cut* are almost clinical in their descriptions of what leads girls to cut, how it relieves stress, and the kind of help that is available. Steven Levenkron, author of *The Luckiest Girl in the World*, is a psychotherapist who is, according to the publisher's notes, a national expert on anorexia and other illnesses. His authentic examination of the problem is helpful in dispelling some of the repulsion that often accompanies discussions of self-mutilation. Both books are extremely optimistic in their outlook of the behavior as one that can be stopped by effective therapy. The following questions can help lead classroom discussion about them:

- **Why do Callie and Katie begin to cut themselves? What is it about the cutting that makes them feel better?**
- **What societal or family pressures are Callie and Katie under that make them feel worthless or incompetent?**
- **Who or what friends or family members help the girls to stop cutting themselves? How?**
- **Do Callie and Katie benefit from professional help? How?**
- **What would you do if you had a friend who was cutting herself?**

Sex

There is no doubt that the physical process of sexual engagement is critically important to children approaching and experiencing adolescence. It could be argued that it is a pivotal experience that marks entry into adulthood. The 2003 National Youth Risk Behavior Survey of high school students in grades 9 through 12 indicates that slightly under half, 47%, have had sex, and 14% have had four or more partners (cited in Hollander, 2004, p. 141); 25% of students report using drugs or alcohol before intercourse. Encouragingly, the survey indicates that 63% of high schoolers used a condom during the last time they had intercourse, as opposed to only 46% who reported doing so in 1991, indicating increased awareness of the risks of sexually transmitted disease and teen pregnancy (p. 141).

Sex in Young Adult Literature

Despite teenagers' consuming interest in the subject, few YA books actually center around the issue of sex. This is almost certainly due to resistance on the part of adults to exposing young people to stories of sexual encounters. In fact, the book *Forever* (Blume, 1975), considered by many to be a classic about a girl's first sexual experience, is one of the most heavily challenged and banned books in the United States (American Library Association, n.d.)—but it is still read widely by adolescents.

The book begins with a typical "girl meets boy" scenario in which Katherine, a high school senior, goes to a fondue party and meets Michael, a senior at another school. They begin to date, and by the fifth week of their relationship they are exploring each other's bodies. Michael wants to have sex with Katherine, but she resists at first. She tells her best friend Erica, "I want it to be special," arguing that sex is best if the participants are in love. When Michael invites Katherine to go skiing for a weekend with his family, they have intercourse and declare their love. They are soon focused primarily on sex, which becomes a major part of their relationship. The book frankly describes their sexual encounters, including graphic depictions of genital stimulation and orgasm. With the encouragement of her liberated grandmother, Katherine visits a Planned Parenthood clinic to get information about and a prescription for birth control. Michael and Katherine begin to plan a future together, but it is interrupted when Katherine's concerned parents force her to take a job at a summer camp. Separated from Michael, she becomes attracted to another camp counselor. When Michael comes to visit her at the camp, she is unable to have sex with him and admits that she is involved with someone else. Michael is devastated.

In her autobiography *Letters to Judy: What Your Kids Wish They Could Tell You* (1986), Blume states that she wrote the book at the request of her 14-year-old daughter, who wanted to read something about "two nice kids who fall in love, do it, and nothing terrible happens to them" (p. 204). Her daughter had grown tired of reading novels in which girls who "did the deed" got pregnant or were abandoned and condemned. However, as Trites (2000) points out, the story has many conflicting messages about sex. On the one hand, Blume seems to be showing that it is natural for couples who fall in love to have sex. Both the boy and the girl experience intense physical pleasure during the encounters, and because Katherine acts responsibly and obtains birth control, there are no repercussions. On the other hand, the implicit message of the book seems to be that young love does not last forever and that teenagers are not ready for the kind of intense commitment that sex demands. As Trites explains, Katherine clearly feels guilty while she is involved sexually with Michael. Although the book appears to condone sex that occurs within the context of a loving relationship and is accompanied by appropriate cautionary measures, at the same time it questions it. This may make for a confusing read, but it also makes for a great discussion.

An interesting counterpoint to *Forever* is the much more recent book *Alice on the Outside* (Naylor, 2001), another YA novel whose frank discussion about sex landed it on the list of most commonly challenged books for children (American Library Association, n.d.). In this book, the protagonist, Alice, is in the eighth grade. She has a boyfriend and two best friends, so her life should be ideal, but it is not. The mother of Pamela, one of her friends, has just run off with her personal trainer. Alice and Pamela are obsessed with the idea of sex. The first part of the book describes Alice's attempts to find out what sex is like. Fortunately, she has a divorced older cousin, Carol, who is able to share information with her in a helpful but realistic way. Carol contrasts "movie sex" with "real sex" when she tells Alice, "In the movies, a couple has intercourse, and the man and woman climax at the same time. In real life, some men and women like to make love in other ways" (p. 26).

Yet Carol insists that eighth graders are too young to have sex, telling Alice, "You don't have to think about these things for years yet! It would have been embarrassing for me at fourteen too" (p. 27). Nevertheless, Alice has engaged in heavy kissing on a porch swing by the end of the novel, and Alice's friend Pamela has let a boy touch her breasts, so the underlying message is that sex is on the near, rather than the far, horizon for these eighth graders. This book clearly reflects the concern that many girls begin to explore their sexuality too young. Pipher (1994) writes,

> Today more adolescent girls are sexually active earlier and with more partners.... My own belief is that junior-high girls are not ready for sexual experiences beyond kissing and hand holding. Girls this age are too young to understand and handle all the implications of what they are doing. Their planning and processing skills are not adequate to allow them to make decisions about intercourse. (p. 208)

Another event that tackles a taboo subject in *Alice on the Outside* occurs when Alice is invited to spend the night with her new friend, Lori Haynes. Lori tries to hold hands with Alice and tells her that she likes her in a special way. Alice is sympathetic toward Lori, and later in the book she actively defends her against other girls who call her a "lesbo" and try to shun her. Although this is not a central plot of the book, it is an important one and argues for tolerance of homosexuality. Lori does find a partner and they go to the eighth-grade dance together, although Alice notes,

> I noticed they didn't really touch. They'd dance the fast numbers together with everyone else, but as soon as the slow music came on, numbers where couples put their arms around each other, they'd leave the floor and walk around the gym talking to the other kids. I was sorry they felt they couldn't do the slow dances, but glad they'd decided to come. (p. 163)

More and more books for teens are tackling the issue of homosexuality. The Printz honor book *Hard Love* (Wittlinger, 2001) tells the story of high school junior John Gilardi. John falls in love with beautiful and exotic Marisol, even though she tells him right away that she is a lesbian. John's inability to accept this fact leads him into despair at first, but eventually he reconciles himself to it.

Girls today are surrounded by images of sexuality, both heterosexual and homosexual. Media messages encourage girls to dress provocatively and television shows about teenagers include frank depictions of sexual activity. Pipher (1994) writes,

> Our culture is deeply split about sexuality. We raise our daughters to value themselves as whole people, and the media reduces them to bodies. We are taught by movies and television that sophisticated people are free and spontaneous while we are warned that casual sex can kill us. We're trapped by double binds and impossible expectations. (p. 206)

Discussing books such as *Forever*, *Alice on the Outside*, and *Hard Love* allows girls to clarify these binds and expectations. The following questions may help:

- Why do Katherine and Alice decide to have—or not to have—sex? How are they influenced by their friends' advice and experience?
- What role do parents and other relatives have in the girls' attitudes about having sex?
- What are the messages in the novel about having sex? What consequences are there?
- What are different types of romantic relationships that the book explores? How does sex relate to these relationships?
- If you had a friend that was thinking about having sex, what would you tell her?

Rape and Sexual Abuse

The incidence of rape or attempted rape among adolescent girls is staggering. The 2004 National Crime Victimization Survey indicates that one in six women in the United States has been the victim of completed or attempted rape; about 44% of these women are under age

18, and 15% are under 12. The survey shows that two-thirds of rapes are committed by known assailants: 47% were friends or acquaintances, and 20% were intimate partners or relatives. Unfortunately, less than half of rapes or sexual assaults are reported. Women often do not report these assaults to police because of guilt, shame, and fear of reprisal (Rape, Abuse, & Incest National Network, 2006). The effects of rape are devastating and long-lasting, and can include headache, fatigue, decreased appetite, eating disorder, sexual dysfunction, and suicide attempts. One longitudinal study found that substance abuse among girls who had been raped was more than double that of girls who had not been raped (American Rape Statistics, n.d., para. 32).

Rape and Sexual Abuse in Young Adult Literature

The novel *Speak* (Anderson, 2003), which has been mentioned previously, centers on the rape of a young girl, Melinda. During a summer party, 14-year-old Melinda has too much to drink and allows herself to be led off into the woods by a handsome, charming senior. When he begins to rape her, she is so traumatized that she is unable to fight him off. After the rape, she calls the police but flees before she can be questioned. Melinda tells no one about her rape. The rapist, unfortunately, has emerged from the incident completely unscathed. Melinda has no one to turn to for help in dealing with the trauma. She withdraws from life, hiding in a school closet and finding ways to stay home from school. One of the key events that triggers Melinda's recovery occurs when she writes a warning about the rapist on the bathroom wall and sees many others writing back in confirmation. At the end of the novel, Melinda's attacker tries to repeat the rape. But now, Melinda can scream and fight back, so she prevails.

The novel's portrayal of a rape victim is convincing. Melinda blames herself for what has happened, which is common. She hides her experience, rather than facing it, another frequent behavior. By analyzing the book, girls can clearly see the pitfalls of those reactions. According to *Speak*, the "solution" to the problem of being raped is clearly to talk about what has happened and to garner support from adults and peers. This approach applies to all types of abuse—verbal, emotional, and physical. Both art and gardening are suggested by the novel as possible therapeutic approaches that help girls heal.

Are You in the House Alone? (Peck, 1976) is a story about rape couched within a mystery/suspense format and set in 1970s Connecticut. The narrator, Gail Osbourne, tells her own story about being raped. Gail has been targeted by a sexual predator who happens to be part of a wealthy and successful family. Unlike Melinda, Gail first attempts to bring her rapist to justice, but she discovers the legal difficulties that women face when accusing a rapist. Gail cannot find justice in the courts. Like Melinda, she retreats into herself, blaming herself for not having withstood the attack. This has devastating effects on her psyche. Fortunately, a caring drama teacher helps Gail repair her damaged emotions.

Both Anderson and Peck have spoken forcefully about writing novels that deal with the issue of rape. In one particular interview, Anderson talks about date rape, arguing that there is "no blurry line of rape. If a girl/woman says no, and the boy/man has intercourse with her, it is rape" ("Author Profile: Laurie Halse Anderson, 2005," para. 8). She continues, "Some guys don't take no for an answer because they have always gotten their way.... There are some twisted souls who think raping a girl makes them men. It doesn't. It makes them scum" (para. 8).

Peck (1978) explains that he wrote his book specifically

> to alert young people to this crime, to the legal posture that favors the criminal at the victim's expense, the *necessity* for follow-up medical treatment that few rape victims seek, the attitude of a society that refuses to come to grips with this clear and present danger, the situation that a victim with a previous sexual history encounters in our courts of law. (p. 174)

Although Peck wrote these words decades ago, they still ring true. While he acknowledges that adults are conflicted about the extent to which they want their daughters to know about sexual violence, Peck argues that "there are no books, fiction or nonfiction, for adolescent readers on topics that are not more blatantly aired on TV" (p. 173).

A less frequently addressed issue is sexual abuse by fathers, stepfathers, and other relatives. An excellent novel that addresses this issue is

Chinese Handcuffs (Crutcher, 1989). The protagonist of the book, Dillon Hemingway, is a high school athlete who competes in triathlons. His friend Jennifer is also an athlete. She is suffering in silence, and Dillon knows that something is wrong at home. When Jennifer tries to kill herself, Dillon finally discovers her secret—her stepfather, a lawyer, has been molesting her for years. Dillon is able to help Jennifer with the help of some wonderful adults. Jennifer also decides to go to the prosecutor and try to make her stepfather pay for what he has done.

Girls need to speak about these terrible things that can and do happen. Anderson emphasizes the importance of communication:

> Traumatic events (like death, moving, divorce, abuse, harassment, rape) lead to silence—it is just so painful to think about, you block it. Only you can't block pain. It's like a river—block it one place and it floods somewhere else...You have to talk about things that hurt. ("Author profile," 2005, para. 6)

The following questions can help get students thinking about and discussing these important issues:

- What are the effects of rape or molestation on Melinda, Gail, and Jennifer?
- Who or what friends or family members help the character deal with the rape or molestation? How?
- Are there signs that other characters notice, despite the protagonist's silence?
- What challenges do the characters face when they try to speak up for themselves and get justice? What positive things happen?
- What could you do to help a friend who was raped or molested?

Teen Pregnancy

The media has celebrated the fact that teen pregnancy in the United States declined in the 1990s (MacDorman, Minino, Strobino, & Guyer,

2001; Rubin, 2001). Nevertheless, teen pregnancy continues to be a major issue in the lives of adolescents. An excellent research summary by Kirby (2001) reports that "despite the declining rates, more than four in ten teen girls still get pregnant at least once before age 20, which translates into nearly 900,000 teen pregnancies a year" (p. 3). According to Kirby, teen pregnancy exacts a high emotional cost, especially for younger girls:

> When teens give birth, their future prospects become more bleak. They become less likely to complete school and more likely to be single parents, for instance. Their children's prospects are even worse— they have less supportive and stimulating home environments, poorer health, lower cognitive development, worse educational outcomes, more behavior problems, and are more likely to become teen parents themselves. (p. 3)

Teen Pregnancy in Young Adult Literature

Quite a few novels in recent years have addressed the issue of teen pregnancy, and most describe the experience from the mother's perspective. (One notable exception is the winner of the 2003 Printz Award, *The First Part Last* [Johnson, 2003], which relates the experiences of a teen father.) Two excellent novels that portray the world of the single teenage mom are *Make Lemonade* (Wolff, 1993) and *Like Sisters on the Homefront* (Williams-Garcia, 1995).

Make Lemonade is a fascinating book told in verse form. The narrator, 14-year-old LaVaughn, answers an advertisement for a babysitter on the school bulletin board to make extra money for her college fund. LaVaughn's new employer is a single teen mom, Jolly, who has two children, a two-year-old boy and a baby girl. Jolly has no family because as a teenager she was basically homeless, and the fathers of the children have no interest in them. LaVaughn determines that she is going to help Jolly, and she does. LaVaughn watches Jolly's children when Jolly is at work; then, when Jolly loses her job, LaVaughn babysits the children for free while Jolly looks for new employment. The book emphasizes the incredible difficulties that accompany raising children without a support system. The book shows how social programs help Jolly take control of her life, but also reveals that it is difficult and sometimes demeaning to accept public assistance.

In contrast, *Like Sisters on the Homefront* showcases a teen mother who has a large family. The book begins with 14-year-old Gayle being dragged to an abortion clinic by her outraged mother. Gayle has already had one baby out of wedlock, and her mother is determined that she will not have another. Gayle's mother decides to send her and her infant son, Jose, to relatives in rural Georgia, and Gayle is appalled to find that her uncle and his family are devout Christians with conservative habits. Gradually, Gayle learns to value her loving Georgia family, especially her great-grandmother, and to recognize the shallowness of her former New York life and friends. At the end of the book Gayle stops her cousin, Cookie, from meeting her boyfriend and sleeping with him in an attempt to prevent her cousin from making the same mistakes Gayle did.

Both of these books emphasize the impact of pregnancy on the life of the teenager, sparing no details about the difficulties involved and the sacrifices required. Davis and MacGillivray (2001) studied 17 YA short stories and novels dealing with teen pregnancies, including both of the books mentioned above. Using coding techniques, they identified eight messages that surfaced in the works:

1. Don't have unprotected sex, even once.
2. Most mothers keep their babies.
3. Having a baby may put your education on hold, but you can still achieve your goals.
4. When you are pregnant, you are on your own.
5. For guys, sex is about fun. For girls, sex is about [many complicated things].
6. Young women have to live with consequences; young men don't.
7. Teen pregnancies do not mandate marriage.
8. Teens from "troubled homes," or their partners, are more likely to become pregnant. (pp. 91–97)

Davis and MacGillivray felt that the books they studied were generally realistic and accurate in their portrayals of teen pregnancy. However, they noted that the books tended to ignore discussions of race and class as they related to the subject. Also, they failed to include the description of prenatal care, which is critical in ensuring the health of infants. Finally, the books ignored discussions about birth control as a way of preventing unwanted pregnancies.

Because so many adolescent girls are engaging in or considering sexual intercourse, they are aware of the real dangers of pregnancy. These novels clearly reveal the effect of pregnancy on the course of a girl's life, shaping her voice so that it reflects not only her wants and needs but also those of her infant. The following questions can help start discussion about teen pregnancy:

- Why do Jolly and Gayle get pregnant? What peer or societal forces are influences?
- How could the pregnancy have been prevented?
- Who or what friends or family members help the teenager with the pregnancy, the baby, or both? How?
- How do other adults or professionals help the teen mother?
- Look at Davis and MacGillivray's eight themes: Do you agree or disagree with these points? After reading the book(s), would you add anything to the list?
- What specific challenges do teen mothers in the novels face?
- How do the lives of these teen mothers compare to your own? What do they give up? Do they gain anything?
- What would you do if you had a friend who was pregnant?

Eating Disorders

Chapter 2 discussed how the quest for physical beauty and lookism has pervaded the U.S. psyche. In particular, being thin is currently celebrated as a critical attribute for female models, singers, and stars, even though, ironically, actual figures show an accelerating trend towards obesity in the United States. Statistics show that about 1 of every 100 girls between ages 10 and 20 suffer from anorexia (Anorexia Nervosa and Related Eating Disorders, Inc., n.d.). About 4 of every 100 college-age women have bulimia, although it is difficult to gather accurate information about this disease because many sufferers are able to keep it secret. Without treatment, 20% of people with serious eating disorders die. Twenty percent of those treated will make only a partial recovery and will continue to be obsessed with their weight and eating habits.

Pipher (1994) posits a number of reasons for the pervasiveness of eating disorders in U.S. society. She notes that food is associated in our culture with approval and warmth; food is socially addicting and has chemical properties that actually provide a physical sense of well-being. Girls find that eating can temporarily stave off depression. However, eating results in weight gain, and in American culture fat is anathema. So many girls enter a vicious cycle of eating to feel better, gaining weight and feeling bad about their appearance, then dieting excessively or purging to lose the weight they gain.

Eating Disorders in Young Adult Literature

Although eating disorders are clearly a major concern among adolescent girls today, few novels that we have found are dealing with this topic. Perhaps slow starvation is too grim for even the most intrepid authors. Movies, particularly those made for television, seem more likely to tackle the subject. However, *Fat Chance* (Newman, 1996) deals with the issue of bulimia. The book is narrated as a series of fictional diary entries written by eighth-grader Judi Liebowitz, who is disgusted with herself for weighing 128 pounds and not looking like gorgeous Nancy Pratt, who has a perfect face and body. Judi decides to diet, but instead of losing weight she gains even more. Her clothes don't fit, and she feels freakish. The more she despairs, the more she eats.

Judi tries starving herself, but nothing seems to work. One day, while hiding out in the girl's bathroom, Judi overhears the sound of someone being sick. It turns out to be gorgeous Nancy Pratt, who explains to Judi that she purposefully purges so she will not gain weight. Judi decides that she can do this, too. Although she loses a little weight, she feels terrible. The story takes a serious turn when Nancy Pratt passes out after purging and is hospitalized. Visiting her, Judi realizes how ill Nancy is and begins to be afraid. A counselor speaks at Judi's middle school about eating disorders, presenting a grim picture of what they do to the adolescent body. In an act of courage, Judi gives her diary to her mother to read. Judi's mom finds the counselor who spoke at the school, and Judi begins therapy. The book is frank about the seduction of bulimia but encouraging about the chances for recovery.

The Earth, My Butt, and Other Round Things (Mackler, 2003) is a wonderful look at what it is like to be a butterball in a family of carrot sticks. At the beginning of the novel, sophomore Virginia Shreves is having a rough year. Her best friend, Shannon, has moved to Washington, and she does not have any other friends. Her beautiful older sister has joined the Peace Corps, and her handsome older brother Byron is attending Columbia University. Her slim, successful parents are rarely around because they are busy with their careers and golf. Virginia begins to diet to fit the expectations of her family and peers. But something unexpected happens: Byron, the perfect child, is expelled from Columbia for date rape. Virginia gradually realizes that beauty really is only skin deep. With the support of her friend Shannon, a sympathetic English teacher, and a boy who is romantically interested in her, Virginia starts to assert her individuality. She pierces her eyebrow and dyes her hair purple. She takes up kick boxing to deal with her anger toward her nonsupportive family. She also discovers that one of the most popular girls at her school is bulimic, and Virginia watches her deteriorate in health, energy, and popularity. By the end of the novel, Virginia is able to write,

> I've never been a fan of my butt. Too big, too round, blah, blah, blah. But when grooving outside the MTV studios in Times Square, it's much more fun to shake your booty when you actually HAVE a booty to shake, not just a bony excuse for a rear end. (p. 239)

Both of these books deal honestly with the shame and despair that girls feel when they are unable to control their weight. They also offer realistic views of how difficult it is to overcome eating disorders, and the different ways that girls can overcome these serious diseases and learn to love their bodies. The following questions may help lead a discussion about books that deal with eating disorders:

- Why are Judi and Virginia unhappy with their bodies?
- How do friends and family members make them feel better—or worse—about their looks?

- Who or what helps the character come to terms with her weight and shape? How?
- To what extent do you think that you should diet, exercise, and use makeup to change your looks? What about plastic surgery?
- Can you think of healthier ways to adjust your appearance?
- What are other body characteristics to be proud of, other than weight or appearance? How do eating disorders adversely affect these good characteristics?
- What would you do if you had a friend who was anorexic or bulimic?

Family Dysfunction

The so-called traditional family of the United States has dramatically changed. As of 2004, only two-thirds of children in the United States lived with both parents; 28% lived with only one parent, and 4% lived with neither parent (Forum on Child and Family Statistics, 2006, para. 2). In 2000, 2.4 million grandparents were primary caregivers, the number of single fathers had increased to over 2 million, and between 6 and 10 million children lived with gay, lesbian, and bisexual parents (Women's Educational Media, n.d.). Because of the large percentage of marriages that end in divorce, more than half of Americans today have lived or will live in stepfamily situations (Women's Educational Media, n.d.).

Probably the most common family crisis experienced by children today is divorce, which ends half of all marriages in the United States (Women's Educational Media, n.d.). Divorce can have devastating effects on children, including behavioral and emotional problems, increased risk of suicide, and increased risks for health problems (Fagan & Rector, 2000). Children between the ages of 12 and 15 who are affected by divorce display two typical reactions: (1) a resistance to growing up, with consequent childish behaviors; or (2) an attempt to accelerate the pace of adolescence, with consequent behaviors for which they may not be physically or emotionally ready. The emotions that accompany these reactions often include loneliness, depression, loss of self-confidence, and increased aggression (Fagan & Rector, 2000). Many times, early sexual activity and substance abuse follow.

Most critically, teenagers need their caregivers to be there for them. It is interesting that Nilsen and Donelson (2005) cite a recent news article that states 75% of teenagers surveyed reported that they "really liked their parents and wanted to have more to do with them" (p. 124). The second part of the statement is striking because it implies an inability of teenagers to access and connect with their parents.

Family Dysfunction in Young Adult Literature

The reverberations of family dysfunction on young girls can be seen in a number of novels. *Run for Your Life* (Levy, 1996) features 13-year-old Kisha, who lives in the projects with her mom and dad and her brother Ty. Her mom and dad seem to get along, although Kisha's dad has been out of a job for several years and the family lives on welfare. But when Kisha's mom gets a job at the local school, the marriage begins to fall apart. Finally, in a rage, Kisha's dad shoots and wounds her mother. Kisha and Ty are devastated, and Kisha cannot imagine ever forgiving her father or reuniting as a family. The fragile family structure is contrasted with the strong running team that Kisha has joined and the support that she enjoys from her teammates and coach.

Another excellent series that explores family dysfunction is the Tillerman Saga, by Cynthia Voigt. In the first novel, *Homecoming* (2002), a mother abandons her three children in a shopping mall—the ultimate betrayal. Terrified, the children make their way to various unknown relatives, seeking a place that will take them in. Finally, they arrive at their grandmother's and redefine what it is to be a family. Dicey, the sibling who leads them, is the protagonist in the series and must alternate between being a mother, a sister, and a child.

Both Kisha and Dicey have parents who fail them and cause them to seek other structures for support. In doing so, these characters develop a strong voice. Unfortunately, many teens are not so fortunate. The support of other adults, and sometimes peers, is often critical in allowing girls to develop their voices in the absence or dysfunction of parents. Novels allow girls to explore who these surrogate parents and families can be, and the following questions can help gain further insight into this topic:

- **How do the problems that parents in the novel are facing affect the teenage character(s)?**
- **Who or what friends or family members provide the support that the parents do not provide? How?**
- **What would you do if a friend of yours were having family problems? What kinds of behaviors or attitudes might be warning signs?**
- **Can you think of other adults or professionals who could provide love and support to a teen living in a family with many problems?**
- **What are the different types of families that *are* functional? (Keep in mind that *family* means many different things.)**

Physical Abuse

The darkest side of family dysfunction involves the issues of physical abuse and neglect. Although it is difficult to gather consistent and reliable data, it is clear that many adolescents experience abuse of one form or another. Noring (2000) shares data revealing that in 1996, three million children in the United States were reported as abused or neglected—a 44% increase since the previous data collection in 1986. An overwhelming majority of these children were from poor households. Shockingly, Crabtree (2003) reported that a recent Gallup poll found that over one-third of teenagers (36%) knew a peer who had been physically or sexually abused.

The effects of abuse are traumatic for both boys and girls. Studies have shown that victims of abuse are more likely to be depressed, have difficulty functioning, be violent, and run away (Bao, Whitbeck, & Hoyt, 2000; Kaplan et al., 1999).

Physical Abuse in Young Adult Literature

Staying Fat for Sarah Byrnes (Crutcher, 2003; discussed also in chapter 2) tells the story of two friends, Marty and Sarah, who are both ostracized throughout their school years—Marty because he is so fat and Sarah because she was horribly disfigured in an accident. Despite their physical handicaps, both are bright and funny, and they have banded together against teasing, ridicule, and hypocrisy. At the beginning of the book, Sarah becomes catatonic and is admitted into a mental hospital. Sarah seems unable to communicate, but gradually we learn that she is faking her condition to escape her abusive father. Sarah finally reveals that her childhood "accident" involving hot oil was actually a deliberate act by her father to punish her mother. Sarah has endured constant verbal abuse and threats of more physical abuse since that time. Marty is stymied in his efforts to extricate Sarah from her horrible home life, but he helps Sarah locate her mother, who is so traumatized by spousal abuse that she refuses to do anything. Finally, some caring adults take charge of the situation, and Sarah is rescued.

Although the topic is difficult, teenagers respond positively to stories about abuse. According to one of our college students, middle school students she observed reading *A Child Called "It": One Child's Courage to Survive* (Pelzer, 1993), a graphic description of an abused boy, were extremely engaged in the story. Some students shared their own experiences, while others expressed sincere gratitude for the way their parents treated them. Again, these books provide a safe forum in which students can discuss a topic that is otherwise considered taboo. The following questions may help students to think about ways in which they can escape abusive situations and ways to help friends explore these options:

- **In what ways does the abuse that Sarah Byrnes suffers affect her ability to express herself?**

- **Who helps Sarah to deal with the abuse? Who prevents Sarah from dealing with the abuse? How do these people affect Sarah's development of an authentic voice?**

- What would you do if you had a friend who you suspected was being abused? What are some of the warning signs you should watch for? Do you know of any additional support people you could turn to?

Coping With the Death of a Parent

In compiling writings about teenage girls for her book *Ophelia Speaks*, Shandler (1999) noted that many submissions dealt with a death in the writer's family. According to Shandler, more girls wrote about losing a parent than any other family member, commenting, "Death had intruded on their adolescence, robbing them of youthful innocence and leaving a lasting impression" (p. 120). Upon losing a parent, children experience intense emotion and pain that pervades their childhood. For adolescents, this can result in a sense of loss of self in addition to the loss of a parent (Trimel, 2000). Many adolescents hide their emotions, but then"cry in their room alone" (para. 14).

Death of a Parent in Young Adult Literature

One of Those Hideous Books Where the Mother Dies (Sones, 2004) combines humor and tragedy, as evidenced by the title. The book, written in free verse, describes what happens when 15-year-old Ruby loses her mother. She is sent to live with her absentee father, who is a mega-movie star living in Los Angeles next door to actress Cameron Diaz. Although much of the grief and pain caused by the loss of her mom is eclipsed by the Hollywood glitz of her new life, Ruby writes about how much she misses her mother, and even tries to e-mail her. The e-mails are some of the most touching and revealing parts of the book, showing how much Ruby longs for her mother's presence, as well as the mix of anger and grief that she feels over her loss.

Walk Two Moons (Creech, 1996) is a compelling story of a girl who loses her mother, although the reader does not find out that her mother has died until the end of the novel. Thirteen-year-old Sal's mother has walked away from her family at the beginning of the novel, and Sal takes a trip with her grandparents to try to find her mother and bring her back. As they drive, Sal tells them the story of her unconventional friend Phoebe, who also feels like she has been abandoned by her mother but is able to reconnect with her. The layers of story deal with loss, grief, and acceptance. At the end of the novel, Sal reflects:

> Phoebe and her family helped me, I think. They helped me to think about and understand my own mother...for a while I needed to believe that my mother was not dead and that she would come back. (p. 377)

Both of these stories are powerful and moving. They allow girls to walk in the shoes of those who have lost their mothers through death and abandonment. They provide rich material that enables readers to talk and think about loss, grief, and acceptance. Grace Christ, an author and expert on child bereavement, has written about what children go through when they lose a parent (Trimel, 2000). She emphasizes the importance of helping students understand the nature of death and dying, as well as the grieving process. She reports that, fortunately, over 80% of children are able to resume normal functioning within a year of losing a parent, although children carry permanent emotional scars from early loss. The following questions may help lead a class discussion about a novel that deals with the death of a parent:

- **How does losing her mother affect Ruby? Sal? Do they become different people?**
- **How does losing a parent affect Ruby's and Sal's ability to form new relationships?**
- **What friends or family members help each character deal with her grief? How?**
- **What new things do Ruby and Sal learn about themselves as they come to terms with their loss?**
- **What would you do if you had a friend who lost a parent? What adults or professionals might be available to help?**

Summary

It is no secret that adolescent girls have many concerns weighing on them, including, but not limited to, the issues outlined in this chapter.

The books that we have described in this chapter, in addition to accurate information about relevant issues, need to be accessible to girls to help them explore and negotiate the pressures they face. A teacher who is committed to helping girls (and boys) tackle questions about who they are, what they believe, and what they value by using works of contemporary realistic fiction has many options about how to incorporate these works into a classroom lesson. The sample lesson that begins on page 82 puts into action one idea that may engage girls in discussing issues they face. This particular lesson structure, using the novel *Stargirl* (Spinelli, 2002), identifies forces at work on identity and helps guide discussion and deal openly with sensitive topics. Both private and public writing are used to help students share their thoughts.

SAMPLE LESSON PLAN

Lesson Topic

Expression and Suppression of the Female Voice Within and Beyond Jerry Spinelli's *Stargirl*

Lesson Objectives

- Students will learn the value of expressing one's authentic voice and the forces that work against such expression.
- Students will learn to compose a character analysis essay with the purpose of self-discovery.

Instructional Materials

Class set of *Stargirl* (Spinelli, 2002); expression/suppression framework (see Figure 1) on transparency; overhead projector

Activities and Procedures

Whole-Class Discussion (25 minutes)

Introduce the expression/suppression framework to the class, clarifying the concept of a person's *authentic voice* and presenting the idea for class consideration that expression of this voice might be more difficult for female adolescents than for male adolescents (at the same time, acknowledging that it is usually difficult for both). Use this idea as a lead-in to a discussion of *Stargirl*. (Although labeled here as "Whole-Class Discussion," this discussion could include more comfortable conversations in groups of two and three, as well.) Examine the expression/suppression framework as it relates to the novel, and cross out those influences that do not affect Stargirl (as far as we, the readers, know). Following are examples of question strings to generate discussion, presented with further teaching instructions in italics and possible student responses in quotes:

<u>Being Different</u>

- What are some adjectives that describe Stargirl? *Write student responses on the board.*

- What are some things Stargirl does—some specific events from the book—that lead you to believe she is [student-supplied adjective]? *Insert examples from the student-supplied adjectives on the board.*

- Is it an act of kindness if the person receiving it does not interpret it as kindness? Why might the other person not want it? Who has the problem in this situation?

- All told, before the "shunning" takes place, what do Stargirl's peers think about her? *Draw attention to Leo's, "[W]e like having her around" (p. 25), and to the rain waking the mud frogs (p. 40).*

Empowered Female

- Historically, in U.S. culture, what has been the defining characteristic of a successful woman? *Lead students through discussion to conclude that in U.S. society motherhood is perceived as one of the most prevalent characteristics of a successful woman. Consider all students responses, write them on the board, and discuss these as necessary.*

- What are some adjectives that describe a good mother? *Write student responses on the board and discuss.*

- Would you describe Stargirl as empowered? What does she do to make you think this? *Draw attention to any of Stargirl's missions to encourage others, to take care of others (especially the injured basketball player), or to empower all her peers to be themselves.*

- Do you think the ending is realistic? Why, or why not?

- How would the ending be different if Stargirl were a student at our school?

Girlfriend and Boyfriend

- What makes someone a good girlfriend? Is Stargirl a good girlfriend? *Write student responses on the board.*

- What makes for a good boyfriend? Is Leo a good boyfriend? *Write student responses on the board.*
- How much overlap is there between our expectations from a girlfriend and a boyfriend? *Compare what you've written on the board for above responses.*
- What can we say about Stargirl and Leo's relationship?
- Who is the stronger character? Why?
- In what ways does Stargirl help Leo find his voice? *Students will discover that Leo, over time, comes to see the world more like Stargirl does, and he learns that it's important to be yourself.*
- What did you think about Leo's becoming one with the rat? *Lead students to give Leo's experience of losing the boundary between himself and the rat as a microscopic example of what Stargirl must feel: connected with all people.*
- What does Leo give Stargirl? *Emphasize that Leo works to suppress Stargirl's voice yet he is the one who loses; refer to the bittersweet final pages of the novel.*

Private Writing: Journal (30 minutes total, 20 for writing and 10 for sharing)

Explain to students that the answer to these questions are subjective and rely on self-reflection about not only what they believe and value but also how they express their beliefs and values and the extent to which they allow other people to stifle them. Keeping this in mind, ask students to answer these five questions in their journals:

1. Who am I?
2. What do I believe?
3. What do I value?
4. How do I express my beliefs and values to other people?
5. How do I allow other people to suppress my beliefs and values?

Now ask if the students had any insights while writing this journal entry that help them better understand the novel. Ask them if they would like to share with the class.

Public Writing: Character Analysis (20 minutes)
*Note: This portion of the lesson could be adapted to suit writing cur-
riculum requirements. For example, you could alter the assignment to
writing a persuasive letter on either (a) the advantages to society of
being different, or (b) a call for girlfriend empowerment. The idea is
to take a familiar form (such as character analysis or persuasive essay)
and allow students to realize that its usefulness can transfer to a more
personal purpose.*

Instruct students to draft a six-paragraph character analysis of
someone they know who they believe truly expresses his or her original, authentic voice—a Stargirl or Starboy they have met. This will
be a rough draft that is to be revised for homework.

In the essay, students must identify three things that the person believes or values (character traits) and find examples from the life of
that person (plot) that provides evidence of these beliefs and values. If
the person has encountered specific obstacles and has overcome them,
these should be included, too. A frame for the essay might look like this:

Paragraph 1—Who is the person (use pseudonyms)? Describe his
or her age, occupation, etc. What is it about this person that makes
him or her unique/different/unusual?

Paragraphs 2, 3, and 4—Describe one observable character trait
per paragraph, and explain how it reflects the person's beliefs
and values.

Paragraph 5—Detail obstacles the person has encountered. How
has he or she overcome these obstacles?

Paragraph 6—Conclude with a summary of the main points and
the effect this person has had on the writer.

Before students begin writing, share a character analysis that you
have written about a unique person so students have a model to follow. Give students time to complete revision and final drafting of their
writing as a homework assignment.

Closing Activities (10 minutes)
Ask students to share with a partner any successes and difficulties they
have encountered with the character analysis writing assignment.

Invite students to read aloud their work at the beginning of class on the day the final paper is due.

Evaluation

Check student notebooks to ensure they have completed the private writing activity. Assess the final draft of the character analysis writing assignment to ensure clear organization of thoughts; elaboration of key points; use of interesting word choices, vivid examples, and sentence variety; and correct grammar and mechanics.

CHAPTER 4

Something Old, Something New: Girls' Issues in Historical Fiction

Valerie Smith teaches eighth-grade English language arts at a large middle school in the downtown area of a small city. Most of her students live in households of low socioeconomic status, and many are nonreaders. Valerie has found that using literature circles, where groups of students read the same book and discuss it in small groups, has really motivated her students to read.

Valerie has a particular interest in historical fiction. She finds that her eighth graders, who are studying U.S. history, seem to have little understanding of the past until they read about it in a trade book. At that point, the historical context comes alive for them, and the students get excited about the connections they make between history and literature. Many of the historical novels that Valerie uses tell the stories of people who overcame difficult situations, and this seems to resonate with her students because they, too, face poverty and family dysfunction. The stories offer hope that even grave difficulties can be overcome.

Valerie has always been interested in literature about girls, particularly girls in history. She also has had special concerns about the girls she teaches. From their journal entries, she knows that many of them are in crisis. Some are pregnant, some are abused, and many others are simply caught in unhappy family situations and trying to be adults without much guidance or support. Until now, she has never really thought about using literature to help her students tackle some of these issues. Because her interest is in historical fiction, Valerie begins to look at the books on her bookshelf to see if there are any that might offer girls the opportunity to analyze their experiences.

EDUCATORS HAVE long favored historical fiction as a genre ideal for children and young adults to read. Its portrayal of past times and places carries clear instructional benefits, enriching the teaching of history with adventure, romance, and interesting characters. The underlying presumption of this attitude is highly debatable: Many adults believe that history is inherently uninteresting to young people, who supposedly do not relate to the experiences of people who lived in the past and cannot connect with them by studying the broad sweep of history. Adults thus sometimes hope that historical fiction will make history palatable to undiscriminating young tastes.

Certainly historical fiction makes history come alive in that it demonstrates historical events from the perspective of a character that young readers come to know and care for during the course of the novel. Good historical fiction moves beyond the mere introduction of factual material: It reconstructs the past both materially and emotionally, showing the impact that major social and cultural events had on the lives of people at the time. For instance, the rapid increase in factory mills early in the Industrial Revolution, the Dust Bowl of the 1930s on an Oklahoma farm, and the yellow fever epidemic in Philadelphia in 1793 all had profound effects on human life. As the young protagonists in these stories experience conflicts between their desires and the historical situations that surround them, young readers experience history in a more dynamic form than most textbooks offer.

To qualify as good historical fiction, novels must meet certain criteria. Nilsen and Donelson (2001) argue that good historical fiction will have the following features:

- A setting that is integral to the story
- An authentic rendition of the time, place, and people being featured
- An author who is so thoroughly steeped in the history of the period that he or she can be comfortably creative without making mistakes
- Believable characters with whom young readers can identify
- Evidence that even across great time spans people share similar emotions

- References to well-known events or people or other clues through which the reader can place the happenings in their correct historical framework
- Readers who come away with the feeling that they know a time or place better. It is as though they have lived in it for at least a few hours (p. 239)

The requirements go well beyond simply avoiding anachronisms or providing a window dressing of costume and landscape; the best historical fiction also captures the social mores and attitudes of the time and faithfully portrays characters' cultural perspectives, which may differ radically from those of contemporary readers. Good historical fiction must strike a delicate balance: It must emphasize universal human emotions while depicting cultural differences in a manner that invites understanding and appreciation.

Expression vs. Suppression: The Quest for Voice in Historical Fiction

Historical fiction presents real opportunities for present-day girls to situate themselves as observers rather than participants in looking at girls' issues. The search for a girl's authentic voice was much more difficult in the past. In the United States of the past, social roles were distinctly gender based in ways that differ widely from those of contemporary gender roles. Depending on the time period depicted, a female protagonist in a historical novel may face restrictions in dress, manners, or behavior; her career and marriage options may be limited according to her race or class. Many girls in the past accepted their roles with equanimity: They grew up surrounded by the social mores of their time and may have felt great satisfaction in fulfilling the expectations of their families and guardians. Yet socially circumscribed roles inevitably compelled other young women to suppress whatever private desires they possessed that conflicted with familial and societal expectations. No doubt a few girls found ways to resist cultural conformity, but they likely made up a small (and probably not socially respectable) minority. Given that one aim of good historical fiction is to represent past social mores and experiences authentically, most good historical novels should depict the experiences of average girls of the time. Thus one might expect that the protagonists would either be girls who accept their public roles happily, or girls who feel they have to follow cultural scripts in their public lives, however conflicted they may feel with their authentic private selves.

However, one seldom encounters either of these types of girls as a protagonist of contemporary young adult (YA) historical fiction. The happy conformist does not work well as a heroine, of course, because there is seldom enough conflict within her role to make her an interesting character. The girl who suppresses her private desires is certainly replete with conflict, but the ending of such a protagonist's story violates the optimism generally considered a hallmark of YA literature; such a denouement would be more likely in a novel written for adults. Instead, as Brown (1998) has observed, while the protagonists of YA historical novels "are often rendered powerless, not only by their youth, but by gender, race, or class, [and] are frequently victimized by greed, hatred, or persecution, nonetheless, they manage to triumph in the face of overwhelming odds" (p. 7). A girl whose story ends with her repressing her authentic self to present a culturally acceptable, but false, public persona would obviously not demonstrate the "triumph" that is usually necessary to most mainstream YA fiction. Authors of historical fiction usually strive to find roles for their female protagonists that meet the demands of the YA literature genre and will appeal to contemporary readers. These heroines experience tensions brought on by their historical roles but satisfactorily resolve these conflicts.

Writers certainly are aware of the difficulties that the constraints of the historical time period impose on their heroines' actions and development. When writing historical fiction, authors must decide how to negotiate the disparity between past and present modes of expected female behaviors so their readers will find the heroines' problems and solutions relevant to their own experiences. Thus, a third kind of female YA protagonist, one who successfully resists the pressures of cultural conformity, has great appeal to both contemporary writers and readers of historical fiction. Brown (1998) acknowledges the literary appeal of such heroines, simultaneously pointing out the difficulties that accompany the creation of these characters:

Katherine Paterson has said, "The characters in history or fiction that we remember are those who kicked against the walls of their societies." The result, a character of heroic proportions, is immensely satisfying to young readers. But there are risks in creating such characters: by inflating their valor and courage, an author may diminish or even sacrifice their humanity, as well as challenge the reader's suspension of disbelief. (p. 8)

There are some critics who disagree with such "wall-kicking" heroines, however. MacLeod (1998) complains specifically about how much recent historical fiction has portrayed women who are exceptions. She argues that focusing on such atypical historical examples of young women undermines the authenticity of historical fiction and presents a false picture of the very real and complex problems that women of the past faced:

> ...therein lies the difficulty I find with these historical novels of the last twenty years. They evade the common realities of the societies they write about. In the case of novels about girls or women, authors want to give their heroines freer choices than their cultures would in fact have offered. To do this, they set aside the social mores of the past as though they were minor afflictions, small obstacles, easy—and painless—for an independent mind to overcome. (para. 14)

In many ways, such well-intended but fallacious portraits of women's experiences are a disservice to the courageous women of history, both those who found ways within cultural expectations to lead fulfilling and authentic lives and those who truly suffered to make changes so their daughters might have a wider range of choices. These inaccurate views ultimately fail to help young readers understand that the experiences of those women of the past and their struggles against very real social restrictions still apply to the issues that young women face today.

Examples of Historical Fiction for Classroom Use

The question arises, then, How can students learn to determine how realistic and reasonable a historical novel is in terms of its presentation of girls' dilemmas and the solutions at which they arrive? Exposing students to a variety of historical novels that offer a range of female character types can teach them to distinguish heroines who negotiate plausible and satisfactory ways to uphold their authentic selves from heroines whose action and decisions are more fantastic and less plausible. We will examine 10 commonly taught historical novels that show a spectrum of possibilities. At the least-plausible-character end of the spectrum, we've placed *The True Confessions of Charlotte Doyle* (Avi, 1992), *The Witch of Blackbird Pond* (Speare, 1958/1977), and *Catherine, Called Birdy* (Cushman, 1995). At the most-plausible-character end of the spectrum, we've placed *Lyddie* (Paterson, 1991), *A Northern Light* (Donnelly, 2003), and *Out of the Dust* (Hesse, 1997). In the middle we found an interesting compromise: Books in which protagonists violate the cultural norms of their times but make plausible decisions because of extenuating historical circumstances. These include *Island of the Blue Dolphins* (O'Dell, 1960) and *Fever, 1793* (Anderson, 2002).

Interesting But Implausible Female Characters

The True Confessions of Charlotte Doyle (Avi, 1992), *The Witch of Blackbird Pond* (Speare, 1958/1977), and *Catherine, Called Birdy* (Cushman, 1995) are enormously popular novels among female readers, no doubt in part because their lively protagonists are all young women with whom contemporary girls can easily identify. The protagonists—Charlotte, Kit, and Catherine—all share a sense of restriction, chafe under the limitations imposed on them because they are female, and rebel against social requirements.

The first book's main character, Charlotte Doyle, starts out as the most conservative of the three books' heroines, yet she goes the furthest in casting aside social expectations. As this Newbery Honor book opens, 13-year-old Charlotte is embarking alone on a trans-Atlantic voyage in 1832 under the care of Captain Jaggery. Charlotte is initially charmed by Jaggery, with whom she identifies because they are both members of the upper class; she fears the ship's lower-class crew, whom the captain encourages her to shun. However, Charlotte strikes up a friendship with the black cook, Zachariah. Charlotte discovers that the crew intends to mutiny, and she informs the captain. When Captain Jaggery reacts violently, punishing Zachariah by having him flogged almost to death, Charlotte renounces her social position, dons male dress, and becomes one of the crew, doing all the work required of the men. After one of the mates is killed during a storm, Jaggery tries to get revenge on Charlotte by trying her for murder, stressing her "unnaturalness" (p. 178). After Jaggery falls overboard and dies in pursuit of Charlotte, the crew votes Charlotte their captain. Charlotte and the crew manage to guide the ship to its destination in Massachusetts. Upon her return home, Charlotte returns to her normal dress but discovers she cannot abide the restrictions her family expects of her. She runs away from home and returns to a life at sea.

Clearly, this story is implausible. First, it is unthinkable that a young girl would travel safely in the company of only male sailors in the 1800s, no matter what the circumstances. Second, it defies belief that she would join a group of mutineers against the captain of a vessel. And third, it is difficult to believe that a young girl of this time with no athletic experience or sea training could do the incredibly demanding physical work required of a sailor. So why is the book so popular despite its improbable plot? Because its protagonist, Charlotte, is spunky and embodies the motto of some present-day feminists: I can do anything you can do—and I can do it better.

For the purpose of discussing girls' issues, however, this novel shows the many voice-suppressing restrictions placed on young girls in the 1800s, and it raises some interesting questions. Charlotte rejects the behavior her culture expects and creates a role for herself in an environment reserved for men. To do this, though, she must deny her feminine identity and look and behave like a man. It is interesting, too, that the book is titled *The True Confessions of Charlotte Doyle*: The word *confessions* implies that there is something Charlotte has done that is wrong and for which she will have to be forgiven. An interesting discussion question for this book could be, Why isn't the book's title *The True Adventures of Charlotte Doyle*? Additional discussion questions for this book might include the following:

- What barriers does Charlotte face that girls today do not?

- What makes Charlotte a believable character? What makes her not so believable?

- In what ways does Charlotte express her authentic self? What does she have to sacrifice to do this?

- Charlotte's peers on the ship are all males. How does their influence affect her decisions and development of character? Would she behave differently if she were surrounded by females?

Going back earlier in time, to the era of English settlement of Connecticut Colony (sometime in the early 1700s, from historical references), *The Witch of Blackbird Pond* (Speare, 1958/1977) centers on 16-year-old Kit, who, left destitute after her grandfather's death, travels to Connecticut to seek a home with her Puritan aunt and uncle, although she has never met them. Kit has grown up in Barbados with money, servants, and freedom to play—she has even been taught to swim. Kit finds to her dismay that life in the New England colonies revolves around prayer, church-going, and hard physical labor, and instead of the lovely silk frocks she is used to, Kit must wear homespun cloth.

Kit begins to help her cousin Mercy teach children to read, but she is dismissed when she tries to make the learning fun. Kit's only friend in the town is an old woman, Hannah Tupper, who is shunned by the villagers because of her Quaker faith. Many people believe she is a witch. When the town turns on Hannah, blaming her for an outbreak of sickness, Kit rescues her. As the novel closes, Kit is wooed by two different men: a prosperous merchant, who offers her a life of relative ease, and the son of a ship's captain, who offers her a life of excitement at sea. Kit chooses the seaman, allowing her to bridge the worlds of Barbados and New England.

Again, this novel (although a Newbery Medal winner) is highly suspect in terms of historical authenticity. The idea of a young girl raised in colonial times in the Caribbean traveling by herself to the Americas, then imposing herself on relatives without warning, is unlikely given the restrictions of the time. As in *The True Confessions of Charlotte Doyle*, however, the idea of a female who breaks traditional rules is appealing, and in both books the sea provides the young woman an opportunity to do so. The contrast of the strict Puritan code with the more sensual experiences of British planters in the Caribbean gives this book an authentic feel and makes it interesting to explore. Both settings clearly show the role of women was to be subservient to males, and it was widely believed that women were unable to survive on their own. Probably the most authentic female experience in the book is that of Hannah, who, because of her differences, is banished from the town and ultimately persecuted as a witch. Also, although Kit gains some measure of freedom by the end of the novel, she is only able to do so through marriage, unlike Charlotte Doyle.

Students may want to consider the following questions after reading the book:

- **What makes Kit a plausible character? What makes her implausible?**
- **Kit has several female role models and peers. What does she learn from each of them? And how does what she learns affect her choices at the end of the book?**
- **How does Hannah compare with Kit's aunt, in regard to their support for (or suppression of) the girls' authentic voices?**

Catherine, Called Birdy (Cushman, 1995) is set in what Nilsen and Donelson (2001) refer to as a generalized medieval period in Britain that has been created from Camelot-type stories of knights, tournaments, ladies, and so on; however, it probably bears little relation to actual living conditions of the time because it focuses on the wealthy class, which was a miniscule amount of the population. The book is written as a diary, which calls its plausibility into question right away because it is unlikely that women in the year 1290 would have been taught how to read and write. Nevertheless, 14-year-old Catherine has a great deal to say, and much of it is highly amusing. Cushman clearly attempts to bring historical authenticity to the tale through physical details; from the beginning, Catherine complains about her situation: "I am bitten by fleas and plagued by family" (p. 1). She describes her tedious routine as daughter of a country knight:

> Today I chased a rat about the hall with a broom and set the broom afire, ruined my embroidery, threw it in the privy, ate too much for dinner, hid in the barn and sulked, teased the little kitchen boy until he cried, turned the mattresses, took the linen outside for airing, hid from Morwenna and her endless chores, ate supper, brought in the forgotten linen now wet with dew, endured scolding and slapping from Morwenna, pinched Perkin, and went to bed. (p. 3)

The humor and rebelliousness of this teenager are wonderfully entertaining for the reader and contributed to the book's Newbery Honor status. Unfortunately for Catherine, who is nicknamed Birdy, far greater ills than tedium are about to beset her: To increase the family's wealth, Birdy's father wants to marry Birdy to the wealthiest suitor he can find. The book details Birdy's antics as she tries to avoid marrying the different men that she meets and her attempts to escape from what she terms "lady-tasks"—embroidery, pleasant conversation, and simple nursing. Catherine constantly bemoans her restricted life, and her diary entries reveal the harsh truth: In medieval times, women were considered chattel. Her best friend Aelis, who falls in love with Catherine's beloved Uncle George, is forbidden to marry him and is instead married to a 7-year-old duke. Birdy longs for adventure and chases off one suitor after another through oft-hilarious insults or deceptions, such as starting a fire in the privy while one of her suitors is using it. A wise woman, however, tells her that although she has wings, she must learn when to use them. Birdy does everything she can to avoid marrying "Shaggy Beard," a wealthy but uncouth and aged baron her father has chosen for her, but finally she realizes that she is trapped and runs away. She has nowhere to go, however. Deciding that life without family is no life at all, she returns to face her fate. As luck would have it, "Shaggy Beard" has died, and his attractive son Stephen has replaced him as Catherine's suitor. The novel ends with Birdy relating that she is cautiously hopeful about her upcoming marriage.

The novel clearly demonstrates the untenable status of women in medieval times, but Birdy's character is undeniably modern. In the afterword to the book, Cushman admits, "Birdy fought years of training and tradition in opposing her marriage to Shaggy Beard. Most girls would have consented, knowing no alternative" (p. 211). In fact, there is little historical record of girls like Birdy, although it is tempting to believe that they existed. Some questions to lead students to focus on this contradiction include the following:

- What makes Birdy a believable character? What makes her less plausible?
- In what ways is Birdy free to make her own choices? In what ways is she not free?
- How do you feel about the choices she makes throughout the novel and especially at the end?
- Is the ending true to Birdy's character? Do you feel she's compromised her authentic self by marrying Shaggy Beard's son?
- How do other female characters affect Birdy's decisions and actions? How do male characters affect her decisions and actions?
- Can you relate to Birdy's situation? What are some of the expectations or limitations you feel pressured by?

Plausible Female Characters

Another group of books seeks to more accurately situate strong female characters within an historical context. *Lyddie* (Paterson, 1991), *A Northern Light* (Donnelly, 2003), and *Out of the Dust* (Hesse, 1997) explore the dilemmas of girls in the United States, from Massachusetts to Kansas and from the 1840s to the 1930s. In doing so, they clearly demonstrate the constraints that earlier times imposed on girls, thus impairing their opportunities to find their authentic voices.

Lyddie begins on a hillside farm in Vermont in the year 1843. Thirteen-year-old Lyddie is the eldest of four children, her father is missing, and her family is nearly destitute. To pay off the family's debts, Lyddie's mother leases the land and forces Lyddie and her brother,

Charles, to become servants: Lyddie at a tavern, Charles on a farm. On a rare visit to check on her family's farm, Lyddie encounters Ezekial, a runaway slave who is hiding out in the cabin. When Ezekial tells Lyddie, "I hope you find your freedom as well" (p. 41), Lyddie realizes that she is as much a slave as he because she works in the tavern for essentially nothing. She resolves to go to Lowell, Massachusetts, where she has heard that they are hiring factory girls and paying decent wages.

Author Paterson describes in minute, horrific detail the hard daily life of a factory girl in the 1840s. Eventually, Lyddie learns to work the looms and teaches herself to read. When a labor organization demands 10-hour days and better working conditions, Lyddie resists pressure to join; as her family's sole support, she cannot afford to be blacklisted and lose her job. She finally rebels, however, when she catches the factory manager trying to rape another factory girl. She dumps a bucket of water over the manager and is consequently dismissed for being a troublemaker. Alone, Lyddie returns to the farm, which is now owned by Luke, the Quaker son of a neighboring family. He asks for Lyddie's hand in marriage. Instead of accepting this tempting offer, which would allow her to stay on her beloved farm, Lyddie decides to travel to Oberlin College, which is accepting women as students. She realizes that she cares for Luke and hopes that he will wait for her, but she is determined to free herself of ignorance and dependence before marrying anyone.

Lyddie's strength, in terms of its value in fostering discussions among girls, is that it paints a clear picture of the lack of options available to young women in the United States, especially those without prosperous families, in the 1800s. The long, harsh hours and deplorable working conditions of a farm hand, tavern maid, or factory worker are terrifying to most readers. The inability of many girls of the day to better themselves, despite their talents and ambitions, is evident in this novel. Paterson describes Lyddie's search for voice, which she equates with freedom and escape from slavery, as an almost insurmountable task. Because of Lyddie's spirit, however, she prevails. Although most girls of the time "escaped" only through marriage, Lyddie rejects that path as another type of slavery and seeks instead to continue her quest for self-development. Questions that may provoke interesting discussion about this book include the following:

- **What details does Paterson give that enable us as readers to understand what life was like for a working-class girl in 19th-century America?**
- **How does learning to read help Lyddie develop her voice?**
- **Do you agree with Lyddie's decision not to marry Luke at the end of the novel? Why or why not?**
- **Can you relate to any of the pressures Lyddie faces?**

A *Northern Light* (Donnelly, 2003) chronicles the story of Mattie Gokey, a motherless 16-year-old girl who lives in the town of Big Moose Lake in upstate New York during the early 1900s. Mattie dreams of becoming a writer, and this aspiration is fueled by her adored teacher, Miss Wilcox, who helps Mattie get accepted to Columbia University on a scholarship. Mattie fears that her harsh and demanding father will never let her go to the university, however, and she feels constrained by her promise to her dying mother to care for her younger siblings. In the hopes of making money for her education expenses, Mattie takes a summer job as a waitress at the Glenmore Hotel. While there, she finds evidence of a murder that has taken place on the lake. (This murder is an actual historical event, and it is the basis for Dreiser's *An American Tragedy* [1925/2000]). Mattie gradually becomes aware of the sordid side of female experience through her realization that the murder victim, a pregnant young woman, has been killed to preserve her lover's reputation. Mattie's loss of innocence coincides with her increasing desire to pursue her dreams. She realizes that her only hope for happiness is to leave Big Moose Lake and everyone in it, and go to New York and try to find her voice:

> Voice...is not just the sound that comes from your throat but the feeling that comes from your words. I hadn't understood that at first. "But Miss Wilcox, you use words to write a story, not your voice," I'd said.
> "No, you use what inside of you," she said. "That's your voice. Your real voice. It's what makes Austen sound like Austen and no one

else. What makes Yeats sound like Yeats and Shelley like Shelley. It's what makes Mattie Gokey sound like Mattie Gokey. You have a wonderful voice, Mattie. I know you do, I've heard it. Use it." (pp. 361–362)

Mattie's tale chronicles the crippling constraints placed on women in the early 1900s. Her story, which parallels the story of the murdered woman, Grace Brown, shows how few choices women had at that time—especially if they broke societal rules. Even the experience of the admirable Miss Wilcox dramatizes the high cost of nonconformity. Mattie is able to escape her constraints but must give up her family ties and romantic dreams to do so.

Author Jennifer Donnelly has commented, "I feel deeply for generations of women—and men—who did not have my opportunities. My great-grandmother received an eighth-grade education, and then was sent off the farm and into hotel service to help feed her family" (p. 393). Grace Brown, the woman who was actually murdered at Big Moose Lake and whose letters helped to convict her lover-murderer, inspired Donnelly to write the story:

> When I read those letters, I was deeply upset—grief stricken, actually—that such a kind, funny, perceptive, decent girl had been trapped by her circumstances and then murdered because there was no way out of them...I wanted Grace's death...to allow someone else to escape her confining circumstances and live her life, even though Grace herself didn't get that chance. (pp. 391–392)

Questions that may cause girls to confront these feelings include the following:

- How does Mattie's father restrict her choices? How does Miss Wilcox expand them?

- What is the significance of Royal's gift of the Fanny Farmer cookbook to Mattie?

- What is the price that Miss Wilcox pays for her nonconformity? Do present day girls (and women) and boys (and men) also pay a price for not conforming?

Out of the Dust (Hesse, 1997) takes place in the Dust Bowl of Oklahoma during the 1930s. Written as a free-verse diary, the book chronicles the main events of the life of 14-year-old Billie Jo from the winter of 1934 to the autumn of 1937. Through Billie Jo's eyes we see the devastation of the farms that suffered drought and plague during these years. We learn of her personal tragedy: Billie Jo has accidentally killed her pregnant mother and unborn baby brother by throwing a bucket of lit gasoline out the kitchen door without realizing that her mother was coming up the stairs. In trying to put out the fire, Billie Jo has badly burned her own hands, keeping her from playing the piano, her main talent and one of her few sources of pleasure. The despair of Billie Jo and her father nearly destroys them, causing her father to drink and Billie Jo to run away. But like the farming community, Billie Jo finds the strength to survive. Through painful practice, she gradually regains the use of her hands and reestablishes a relationship with her father. Instead of desperately trying to get away from the Dust Bowl, Billie Jo reconciles herself to it. Near the end of the book, she writes about how she learns to play the piano again as her hands heal. She is able to understand that although she has tried to escape from the dust bowl, it is the dust that has created the person she is.

Billie Jo's remarkable acceptance of herself and her conditions is awe inspiring. This beautifully written Newbery Medal-winning novel is remarkable not only in its story and verse narration but also in its firm basis in fact. Author Karen Hesse has said of the book,

> It's almost docu-fiction, in that doing the research led me to newspapers from that time period. I didn't speak to many people, but I did read newspapers from that area. And a lot of the events in the book are drawn straight from the newspaper; I just embellished and pulled in the other research to create the book. But a lot of the characters are based on real people I read about. And of course, I created them to be able to carry out the action of the book. I even used some real names of people I read about, people I didn't think would be harmed. ("Karen Hesse's Interview Transcript," n.d., para. 4)

Questions to focus student discussion about this book include the following:

- **How does Billie Jo come to terms with her life in the Dust Bowl?**

- How is Billie Jo's piano playing a metaphor for developing her voice?
- Why does Billie Jo have to learn to talk to her father at the end of the novel?
- Who or what are the major influences on how Billie Jo sees herself?
- Does she accept the way others perceive her as her true identity?

Billie Jo, Mattie, and Lyddie all represent real girls in history who experienced hardship, lack of opportunity, and oppression of one type or another. The authors of these books have been scrupulous in portraying the difficulties these characters faced. Because of their strong spirits and determination, these girls are able to find their voices and use them to overcome many of the constraints that bind them.

Female Characters Who Escape Traditional Roles in Plausible Ways

The third type of historical novel illustrates the experiences of girls of the past who are temporarily freed from societal constraints because of unique historical events. They are allowed to engage in actions atypical of that time in history, yet because of the unusual social circumstances, the story remains convincing.

Fever: 1793 (Anderson, 2002) tells the story of Mattie, a girl who lives in late 18th-century Philadelphia. The book is based on actual historical accounts of a particularly virulent outbreak of yellow fever that occurred in 1793. Mattie's mother and grandfather run a tavern with the help of Eliza, a freed black woman. At the onset of the novel, 14-year-old Mattie is like any normal colonial girl. She does chores, argues with her mother, and secretly pines for a handsome young artist's apprentice. Soon, however, her life completely turns upside down. Yellow fever strikes Philadelphia, and Mattie's mother falls ill. When hundreds of the city's inhabitants become infected and begin to die, the tavern closes, and anyone who is able to tries to escape the city.

Mattie and her grandfather become ill while fleeing to relatives in the country, leaving her mother in the care of Eliza. They recover and return to the city, only to find that Mattie's mother and Eliza have disappeared. When Mattie's grandfather tries to chase away two burglars, he suffers a heart attack and dies. Completely alone, Mattie manages to locate Eliza, who, with others in the Free African Society, is helping to nurse the ill. Together, Eliza and Mattie help others, and finally the fever epidemic abates. Despite her young age, Mattie takes charge and reopens the tavern as a coffeehouse, an innovation she thinks will improve the business. At last, Mattie's mother returns home, greatly weakened and heavily dependent on Mattie. Throughout this ordeal, Mattie demonstrates strength, courage, and compassion.

Author Laurie Halse Anderson accentuates Mattie's experiences by including quotes from historical sources at the beginning of each chapter. For example, chapter 15 opens with the following passage:

> Wives were deserted by husbands, and children by parents. The chambers of diseases were deserted, and the sick left to die of negligence. None could be found to remove the lifeless bodies. Their remains, suffered to decay by piecemeal, filled the air with deadly exhalations, and added tenfold to the devastation.
>
> —Charles Brockden Brown, *Arthur Mervyn; or Memoirs of the Year 1793* (p. 105)

Mattie's amazing accomplishments—surviving the fever, caring for others, and running the coffeehouse single-handedly—are only possible because of the unique circumstances created by the epidemic. The following discussion questions emphasize this point:

- **How do the extraordinary events of the novel cause Mattie to step outside the normal role of a teenage girl in 18th-century Philadelphia? Do you think she would have been able to find this strength without such unusual circumstances?**

- **How do the adults in this novel support or deny Mattie's growing independence? Give specific examples.**

- What enables Mattie to stand up and take charge of her life at the climax of the novel?

Island of the Blue Dolphins (O'Dell, 1960) is another novel about a girl caught in extraordinary circumstances. Twelve-year-old Karana lives on a small island off the coast of California, where her father is the chief of a small Native American tribe. Their life changes when Aleut hunters invade and kill most of the warriors, including Karana's father. When a ship comes to the island, the tribe decides to abandon their home and seek another place to live. As the ship sets sail, Karana jumps off and swims to shore to be with her brother, Ramo, who accidentally has been left behind. Unfortunately, Ramo is soon killed by a pack of wild dogs, which are native to the island. Totally alone and grief-stricken, Karana struggles to find a way to survive. She finds a way to create and use weapons, although this is taboo for women in her tribe. Finally, a ship of white men land on the island seeking sea otter pelts. Karana realizes that she needs human companionship, and she decides to leave with them.

It must be noted that O'Dell wrote the novel with intended respect toward the cultures portrayed, but Karana's culture is entirely fictionalized and should not be used in lessons about Native cultures for young readers as though it were culturally authentic. Teachers using the novel can and should educate their students about its inaccuracies as well as its strengths. However, this novel's portrayal of a strong female character fits nicely within a discussion of leading girls to find their authentic selves because Karana is driven by her situation to expand her definition of what tasks she can accomplish as a woman, and she finds great pleasure in her achievements. The following questions can help lead a discussion about this book:

- What unusual set of circumstances make it both possible and necessary for Karana to step out of the traditional female role? How does she feel about her unusual role, and why does she feel this way?
- Why does she make friends with the dog Rontu, who killed her brother?

- How does losing her brother force Karana to change the way she sees herself?
- What do you think of Karana's decision about hunting near the end of the book? Do you agree with her or not?
- How would Karana's future be different had she stayed on the boat with her tribe? And how would that compare to her new future with the white people, with regard to her role in society?

Both Mattie and Karana, because of circumstances that leave them unable to depend on males or other adults for survival, assume roles and tasks that are generally forbidden in their societies. They become resilient, fearless, and competent young women, finding strong voices that help them overcome daunting circumstances. There are signs in both of the books, however, that these voices may not remain: As the books end, Mattie talks about a budding relationship and Karana is being measured for a blue dress that will be considered "decent" at the mission where she will be taken. This point could make for interesting classroom discussion, too.

Summary

Reading historical fiction offers girls a great opportunity to learn about past societies that restricted women in different ways. Some historical fiction is quite accurate in the depiction of girls' lives, roles, and options of the time; other historical novels are more playful or imaginative, describing situations in which girls break boundaries in unlikely ways. Historical fiction is particularly helpful in bringing girls to understand how societal forces have shifted in their impact on girls. Then girls can more readily see the way in which their own society exerts pressure on them to behave in certain ways.

Teachers who wish to craft lessons using historical fiction have a wealth of material and resources from which to choose. It is particularly effective to combine the reading of fictional work with an examination of historical documents or artifacts that reveal the times, especially as they affected the lives of women. The lesson plan that begins on page 107 uses the novel *Out of the Dust* (Hesse, 1997) to examine the expectations for adolescent girls in a bygone era, recognizing both differences and similarities between the 1930s and today.

SAMPLE LESSON PLAN

Lesson Topic
Identifying history in historical fiction

Lesson Objectives

- Students will read a poetic novel and demonstrate understanding of literary elements (plot, characters, setting).
- Students will learn how historical events inform historical fiction.
- Students will analyze the female protagonist and identify forces that shape her development.

Instructional Materials
Class set of *Out of the Dust* (Hesse, 1997); access to computers for website search, and printers; construction paper, scissors, and glue

Activities and Procedures

It should take about 10 days to complete this particular novel and corresponding discussion.

Before Beginning Novel
Ask students to rate the top four or five classmates with whom they would like to work. Assign groups based on these ratings and your knowledge of the students' abilities. Groups should be heterogeneous and contain no more than five students each. Develop assignment sheets for each section of the book with teacher-generated questions for groups to answer. (Sample questions are provided throughout the following lesson plan.)

Day 1: Introduction (45–50 minutes)
Introduce the novel by giving a brief description of the historical period. Show students the collection of websites about the Dust Bowl. Make these available for groups to use. Have computers available with printers to print out photographs from the following websites:

American Experience: Surviving the Dust Bowl
www.pbs.org/wgbh/amex/dustbowl
Good film accompanies website, with subpages on historical events and people, an interview with a survivor, a timeline, and maps.

The Living History Farm
www.livinghistoryfarm.org
National Endowment for the Humanities–praised website based on a Nebraska farm. Excellent historical subpages: Click on "Farming in the 1930s," then "Water" to reach the specific section on the Dust Bowl. There are many additional pertinent pages that discuss farm life during the Great Depression.

WERU The Wind Erosion Research Unit, Multimedia Archive
www.weru.ksu.edu/new_weru
Excellent page on the Dust Bowl with 1930s pictures; also pictures of recent dust storms, showing that the problem has not entirely disappeared.

1930s Dust Bowl
www.ptsi.net/user/museum/dustbowl.html
Good brief history with pictures of the dust storms.

Read aloud the first few pages of the novel, using the overhead projector to show each page and grab students' interest. Discuss the form of the book: a series of free-verse poems.

Distribute books and assign groups. Pass out assignment sheets for the first discussion group, outlining pages to read and questions to consider. Each day's assignment sheet should include 5–7 points for discussion. (See Figure 4 for a sample assignment sheet for day one.)

Figure 4   First Discussion Group Assignment Sheet

1. At the beginning of the novel, how does Billie Jo describe herself?
2. What is Billie Jo's relationship with her mother? With her father?
3. In this section, Billie Jo loses Livie, one of her closest friends. How does she handle this?
4. How do you think Billie Jo really feels about Mad Dog? Explain, using text to support.
5. Why is Franklin D. Roosevelt (FDR) significant to this story? Why would Billie Jo's town celebrate his birthday?

Allow students time to read pages 6–16, then let students get into their groups and begin the assignment sheet. One student will be the recorder for the group; this job will rotate each day.

After discussing the questions, the groups will search the websites for 2–3 photos that best illustrate the pages read. They will print these out and paste them on construction paper, creating a scrapbook for Billie Jo. On each page, students will write something that connects Billie Jo to the picture and text. You can do a page, as well, to show as a model.

Days 2–10 (20 minutes for reading; 25 minutes for scrapbook project)
Allow a few minutes at the end of class for groups to summarize what they've read and pose any questions to the class that they wish to talk about more thoroughly.

Repeat this process for every 15–20 pages students read, with assignment sheets that incorporate questions about the challenges Billie Jo faces and the choices she makes, as well as questions about basic information and story elements questions (i.e., character, plot, theme, etc.). While monitoring groups, encourage students to pose their own questions and work as a team to find the answers for those questions. Try to get students to feel ownership of the text and to continually interact with it to find deeper meaning.

On day 7, introduce the idea of expression versus suppression of voice using the expression/suppression framework in Figure 1 (see page 23) to examine how Billie Jo has struggled to find her authentic voice. As part of the day's assignment sheet, ask students to use the text to find evidence of how external forces (i.e., adult influence, society's expectations, etc.) have shaped Billie Jo. At the end of the class, lead a general discussion about these topics.

Day 11: Closing Activities (30 minutes for writing, 15 minutes for sharing)
Students will look over the scrapbook they have created. Ask students to each write a two-page, first-person reflection as Billie Jo, considering what has happened and how she has grown and learned through her experiences. (Have students read the last page of the novel carefully before writing.)

Then students will get back into their groups to share their scrapbooks with other groups (trading them in sequence) to see how other groups have recorded the story.

Evaluation

Assess students on their group assignment responses, scrapbooks, and reflection papers, ensuring that the photographs accurately reflect the story, the written captions tie Billie Jo to the photos, and the writing includes the following: what has happened to Billie Jo, what she has learned, and how and why she has changed.

CHAPTER 5

Fantastic Females: Strong Girls in Fantasy and Science Fiction

Markie Burch is a library/media specialist at a suburban elementary school in Santa Maria, California. She enjoys working with her 600 or so students, many of whom are avid readers. Markie has noticed that the fourth- and fifth-grade girls are increasingly wearing clothes designed for teenagers, using makeup, and focused on the boys in their classes. This worries her greatly. Although these girls are generally successful in school, their energies seem to be spent in conforming to an image of the MTV female, scantily clothed and sexually charged. The books that the girls most frequently ask for are books such as The Clique series (Harrison, 2004a, 2004b, 2005a, 2005b, 2006a, 2006b), which emphasize designer clothes and how to be popular.

Markie feels that she must do something to help the girls in her schools think about the choices they are making. She feels that the contemporary books are appealing but might be too obvious in the messages that they send. She is more interested in an oblique approach to confronting the issues of conformity. She is intrigued by the historical novels but even more interested in the genre of fantasy and science fiction. Every student in the school, it seems, has read and loved the Harry Potter series, so Markie decides to peruse the many fantasy novels in her library, using the selection guide outlined in chapter 2.

As Markie looks through her stacks, she discovers that there are many types of fantasy books that offer girls a message of empowerment. First is the fairy tale, because it has been so important in defining girls' roles in the Western tradition, and modern authors have offered revisions of these tales that challenge those roles. She also finds some modern quest fantasies that portray girls as heroes. Markie looks at many works involving the supernatural, focusing on recent successful books that showcase vampires and werewolves. She is troubled by the paucity of science fiction written for and about girls.

THE GENRE of fantasy, as has been commonly noted, describes the world of the impossible made possible. In fantasy stories, animals talk, the dead return to life, and planets spin out of control. Modern fantasy stems from the oral tradition of storytelling, in which great narrators memorized and recounted exciting tales. Some early fantasy stories that are still taught as part of the Western literature tradition include Homer's *The Odyssey*, *Beowulf*, the legend of Robin Hood, and many versions of the Arthurian legend. Discounting animal tales about characters such as Winnie-the-Pooh and Peter Rabbit, which are primarily attractive to young readers, much of Western fantasy deals with a "noble" class of people—knights, princes, princesses, counts, and so forth—and what happens to them. A common structure of fantasy stories is the "heroic/romantic quest," a framework in which a hero is identified. Usually, the hero is a seemingly normal, even ordinary, person but one with remarkable (sometimes hidden) talents. In the beginning of the story, the hero's destiny is revealed, and a huge task, or quest, is established. The hero may be somewhat reluctant to embark upon his quest, but does. Typically, he is given a token, help, or advice, often by a magical creature or wise person. The hero tackles the quest, making both allies and enemies, and usually falls in love. The story culminates in a final battle, which, of course, the hero wins. At the end of the story, the hero returns home, often with a love interest in tow. It is amazing how many versions of this basic plot work to engage readers. Recent examples of the incredibly successful *Lord of the Rings* films (Jackson, 2001, 2002, 2003) and the most recent *Star Wars* trilogy (Lucas, 1999, 2002, 2005) illustrate how this framework can be fleshed out in myriad ways.

Expression Versus Suppression: The Quest for Voice in Fantasy and Science Fiction

The use of the masculine pronoun in the heroic quest outline above is intentional. Until recently, all heroes in the quest story have been male. Females in fantasy have had little voice, and it used to be unthinkable that a woman would set out on a quest, unprotected by a man, to do battle. In fact, the females in quest stories were often beautiful, passive maidens who waited for rescue—or they were old crones, hags, or wicked evildoers. This has made much of fantasy literature problematic for scholars like us who look to literature as a way to help adolescent girls find their voices. Fortunately, fantasy authors at the end of the 20th century and into the 21st, many of whom are women, have chosen to create stories in which the hero is a girl, and older women are not relegated to villainy or obscurity. These new fantasy stories provide wonderful vehicles for exploring ways in which girls can find self-expression.

Pierce (1993) argues powerfully that children begin their literary experience with fantasy; nursery rhymes, fairy tales, and magical stories are read aloud to them. However, the experience of school and its base in reality lures children away from their early love of fantasy and only a minority of students remain interested in it. This seems to reflect the attitudes we have found in our college classes, mostly populated by young women, over half of whom state that they "hate fantasy." (To be fair, this often changes once they are exposed to modern young adult fantasy novels.) However, for those young people who remain captivated by fantasy, Pierce contends that it fulfills several basic needs. First, young people display idealism. They believe absolutely that the world can and should be a good place. They identify with heroes of fantasy stories who risk all to save the world, and they believe that the world can be changed. Fantasy novels, therefore, reinforce their belief that good should and does triumph. Second, fantasy stories offer a way for young adults to find "a place to belong" (Pierce, 1993, p. 51). Many heroes and heroines in fantasy novels run away or escape from their original setting and create a new world for themselves. This appeals to many young people who have had difficulty finding a place to belong. Most important, Pierce states that fantasy is "a literature of empowerment" (p. 53). Many heroes of fantasy are ordinary; some are even insignificant. Yet they are able to overcome huge obstacles and in combat defeat adversaries who are far more powerful. This sense of empowerment is a key feature in books with female heroes. Fantasy novels can reveal to girls the possibilities of speaking out, leading, and overcoming obstacles—even those that seem insurmountable.

Fairy Tales, Old and Retold

The most commonly known fairy tales originated from European oral tradition as stories for adults, not children. Because they were not written down for years, they were subject to mutation, so various versions of the tales can be found. Once they were written down, fairy tales began to exhibit more stability. The earliest written European fairy tales are generally attributed to Charles Perrault, who wrote a collection of stories in 1697 for the entertainment of the French court (Nodelman & Reimer, 2003). Perrault's stories included versions of "Little Red Riding Hood," "Cinderella," and "Sleeping Beauty." Perrault's audience was not composed of children, although young ladies of the court were welcome to attend readings of the tales. Another French writer, Madame Le Prince de Beaumont, also wrote a collection of tales in 1756 that was clearly designed for young ladies of the court. These stories included embedded lessons about proper behavior. Her collection included the first written version of "Beauty and the Beast." The best-known authors of fairy tales are the Grimm Brothers, who collected and embellished over 200 German folk tales in 1812 (Nodelman & Reimer, 2003), including variant versions of those mentioned above. When Edward Taylor translated the Grimm brothers' tales into English in 1823 and began marketing them toward children, the tales became immensely popular (Nodelman & Reimer, 2003). Hans Christian Andersen's enchanting literary tales, which drew from folk tales, expanded the scope of fairy tales, and attracted even more young readers. Throughout the late 1800s and the 1900s, many European and U.S. children were exposed to fairy tales by reading them at home or at school. The translation of some of the tales into films, particularly the Disney versions in the latter half of the 20th century, has almost guaranteed that every U.S. child knows the stories of Cinderella, Sleeping Beauty, Snow White, and, more recently, Beauty and the Beast and the little mermaid.

In most of the fairy tales that have become popular with U.S. children, young girls exhibit a clear pattern of behavior. Hallett and Karasek (2002) refer to this pattern as that of "damsels in distress." The young women in the stories are uniformly beautiful and helpless. To succeed they must receive some kind of aid, often through magic performed by others, and the only definition of success in the stories is marriage to a handsome prince. Generally, the other women in the stories are hateful to them and try to prevent them from reaching their goal of living happily ever after: Snow White's stepmother poisons her; Cinderella's stepmother and stepsisters force her to work as their servant. Hallett and Karasek point out that this pattern is consistent with the patriarchal societal framework that existed when these stories were created: Women had little hope of subsisting without the protection and financial support of a man because they could not own property. Thus, women had to compete for available males, particularly prosperous ones, creating jealousy and treachery within the female community.

Scholars in the field of feminist literary criticism debate the power of the fairy tale in establishing female gender identity. Stone (2002) examined the debate over whether gender stereotyping exists in fairy tales, pointing out that a number of writers see fairy tales as nonsexist, whereas others condemn many of the tales as promoting negative female stereotypes:

> We can assume from the intensity of the statements both attacking and supporting fairy tales that these stories are regarded as meaningful for both children and adults rather than as merely quaint and amusing. Moreover, fairy tales apparently have the power to affect readers deeply, either negatively or positively, in ways that other forms of children's literature generally do not. The fact that these multilevel stories are usually read early in life when a child is struggling to find a place in the world, and a sexual identity, can be used to support the arguments of both proponents and opponents of fairy tales. (p. 396)

Stone herself conducted a study of 44 children and adults to determine the impact of fairy tales on their thinking. She found that most of the girls and women she interviewed recognized and resented the sexual stereotypes of the fairy tales, particularly the idea that women must be rescued by a prince. She found that even females who rejected the fairy tale heroine's characteristics of passivity, dependence, and beauty felt somewhat guilty and conflicted about doing so. One woman related,

> I couldn't really say whether the impact of the stories is stronger when you're an adolescent or when you're younger; but the impact in both cases was harmful to me, I think, because instead of making me feel confident or able to develop my strengths or anything, they made me feel there was something in me I had to stamp out. (p. 407)

Another woman, a divorcee with three children, explained,

> I remember "Cinderella" and "Snow White." Now I don't think they show the ideal woman—at least not for me, or for my daughter, but I liked them at her age [nine]. It's too glamorous. A man is supposed to solve all your problems. I thought this would be the answer to what I'd been growing up and waiting for. What a bunch of bullshit! Fantasy is okay, but not if it puts patterns into kids' heads about what to expect from life. (p. 410)

Stone is quick to note that fairy tales are only one source of messages about beauty, marriage, and living "happily ever after" since all types of media—including advertising—have borrowed and expanded on these themes. Nevertheless, there does seem to be evidence that fairy tales, as originally written, carry negative messages for girls. Therefore, it is not surprising that modern authors have chosen to rewrite the tales with a more positive spin.

Retellings of "Cinderella"

"Cinderella" is a story that captivates many readers and writers. It has two corollary, universally appealing themes: (1) the rags-to-riches transformation story and (2) the idea that good triumphs over evil. Cinderella rises from servitude to attain a kingdom (or at least to gain a mate who is heir to a kingdom), and her goodness and patience defeats the cruelty and wickedness of her stepmother and stepsisters. This is a great substructure for a story, and it clearly could be used to showcase the empowerment of girls. However, in the original story Cinderella subserviently follows orders and meekly accepts her fate. Only the intervention of a fairy godmother enables her to attend the royal ball, and only her beauty captivates the prince. Several modern authors have taken the core of the story and added elements that change Cinderella's original character.

Just Ella (Haddix, 2001) begins after Cinderella's prince has discovered her true identity and she has agreed to marry him. Because Ella is a commoner, she must be taught how to behave as a princess. Locked in the drafty castle, she is not allowed to do anything for herself but must take lessons in etiquette, religion, and needlework. She is allowed to converse with Charm, as she calls Prince Charming, for one closely chaperoned hour each evening. Ella realizes to her horror that she is bored out of her mind, and misses the chores and tasks that make her independent. When Ella informs Charm that she has changed her mind about marrying him, she is thrown into a dungeon and threatened with rape and starvation unless she relents and marries the prince. Instead of giving in, Ella digs her way out of the castle.

Ella provides a complete counter to the original passive protagonist of the Cinderella tale. She is smart, funny, and determined. She rejects the opportunity to be a princess in favor of performing meaningful work, and she realizes that beauty is a much less valuable virtue than caring, compassion, and idealism.

Ella Enchanted (Levine, 1998) provides another take on the Cinderella tale. At birth, Ella, the daughter of a merchant, has been given the gift of obedience by her fairy godmother. This means Ella cannot disobey a direct order from anyone. This makes her life miserable, especially after her mother dies and her father remarries a vindictive widow with two cruel daughters. When her father loses his wealth, Ella's stepmother forces her to become a servant—and Ella has to obey her stepmother's every command. However, another fairy helps Ella attend balls that are being held to find a mate for Prince Charming—called Char in this story—who is a wonderful young man. Ella falls in love with Char, but when he asks her to marry him, she realizes that her curse of obedience could cost Char his kingdom. Although she wishes to marry him, she manages to resist his command to marry him, breaking the curse. With the curse lifted, Char and Ella are happily wed. After they are married, Ella refuses to become a princess, choosing instead to be appointed Court Linguist and Cook's Helper (p. 231), and travels with her husband to many different lands. This revision of the classic tale offers a completely new look at obedience as being a curse rather than a virtue, challenging the idea that women should be passive and conforming. Like *Just Ella*, it portrays Cinderella as a resourceful, determined, innovative heroine. It also espouses the idea of doing rather than being—Ella would rather do work than be a princess.

A Retelling of "Sleeping Beauty"

"Sleeping Beauty" is another story common in modern society. The image of a beautiful princess, who has been put under a magical spell and can only be awakened by true love's kiss, has generated numerous interpretations and revisions. As Hallett and Karasek (2002) explain,

> The central image of a sleeping princess awaiting the prince who will bring her (and her whole world) back to life has powerful mythic overtones of death and resurrection. On a more human level the image is a metaphor of growing up: in each case, the heroine falls asleep as a naïve girl and awakens as a mature young woman on the threshold of marriage and adult responsibility. For cultural reasons, the metaphor is generally seen as gender-specific, in that sleep denotes the decorous passivity expected of the virtuous young female—a characteristic that undoubtedly attracted nineteenth-century approval of this tale.... By contrast, the young male must demonstrate his maturity through deeds of daring. (pp. 17–18)

Clearly, the story needs to be revised if it is to remove the markers of "decorous passivity" that were so valued in earlier times. One revision of the story is *Spindle's End* (McKinley, 2000), which begins in a familiar way, with the birth of a new princess, Briar Rose, and the awarding of gifts by fairy godmothers. Of course, the last gift is a curse bestowed by an angry fairy, who proclaims that the princess will prick her finger on a spinning wheel and die by her 21st birthday. However, here the tale departs from tradition. Katriona, a village girl who has come to view the naming of the princess, is given charge of Briar Rose and told to hide her. "Rosie" thus grows up in a small village under the protection of Katriona and Aunt, who are both powerful but benevolent witches. Rosie shows no aptitude for witchcraft, but she can talk to animals. She apprentices herself to a blacksmith and becomes a veterinarian. When she finally learns of her destiny as a princess, she is devastated. She and the blacksmith tackle the witch who laid the curse on her and emerge victorious. This involves a fierce battle, but Rosie is able to avoid becoming a princess. She and her best friend exchange places, and the friend goes to the castle to become queen. Rosie continues practicing the occupation she loves, caring for and communicating with animals. She also declares her love for the blacksmith, and it is reciprocated.

The story provides a wonderful opportunity for discussion about choices and finding one's voice. Rosie rejects a life that appears shallow and empty, embracing instead the opportunity to do meaningful work. Rather than being decorously passive in the manner of the traditional Sleeping Beauty, Rosie possesses what literary critics would call agency over her life—that is, she takes control of events, rather than merely letting them happen to her, the precise opposite of Briar Rose of the original fairy tale. Rosie shows that she, not a prince, has the capacity for fighting and overcoming evil. She sets her own course in life, rather than surrender herself to the mercy of destiny.

Examining "Beauty and the Beast"

A third fairy tale that has attracted the interest of modern young-adult novel authors is "Beauty and the Beast." Warner (2002) examines modern fascination with the beast story by exploring two possible interpretations of the juxtaposition of Beauty and the Beast:

1. The Beast represents that which is untamed, wild, and natural; Beauty is that which is domesticated and civilized. As the world evolves, so does a fear of losing one's connection to the

natural world. The Beast, and Beauty's love of it, represents the need to maintain a connection with nature.

2. The Beast represents female sexuality: forbidden, dangerous, and terrifying. Therefore, Beauty's embrace of the Beast emboldens women to embrace their own sexual desires and passions. Modern writers generally agree that the Beast is far more intriguing and engaging than the "candy-coloured human who emerged from the enchanted monster" (p. 422).

Both of Warner's theories suggest that the story's continuing appeal lies in how it symbolizes a woman finding success through authentic expression of her desires.

In the original tale, Beauty's sisters are mean and cruel to her. They blame Beauty for asking her father to get roses for her, which leads the Beast to demand the life of the father or one of the daughters. Because of their meanness, they are turned into statues by a fairy at the end of the story, and only by recognizing their faults can they regain human form. The fairy makes it clear that Beauty's willingness to sacrifice her life, first for her father and then for the Beast, has resulted in her reward. And, of course, the ultimate reward is a handsome, rich young man. This story perpetuates two themes common in fairy tales: (1) the cruelty and lack of support demonstrated by females toward one another and (2) the rewarding of female submission to and sacrifice for male figures.

A modern retelling of this story, *Beauty: A Retelling of the Story of Beauty and the Beast* (McKinley, 1978), follows the fairy tale quite closely but includes some important revisions. First and foremost, Beauty, the youngest of three sisters, is the only daughter who is *not* beautiful. She is quite small and plain. However, she is very bright and a voracious reader. These are the traits that allow Beauty to connect with the Beast: They share a love of books and conversation. Beauty endures the isolation of the Beast's castle by immersing herself in its library, studying languages and reading many different texts. She and the Beast discuss these books and also take turns reading poetry and novels to one another. This emphasis on cleverness instead of physical beauty is sustained until almost the end of the novel when

McKinley cannot resist transforming Beauty into a physical paragon, presumably to match the Beast's reincarnation. Her eyes have turned from "muddy hazel" to "clear amber" (p. 242), she has developed a dimple, and she has somehow added inches to her height. Another major change in the story is that Beauty's sisters are not vain and cruel, but warm and loving. They do everything in their power to help Beauty. This rendition subverts some of the disturbing messages of girl as victim in the original fairy tale, but it inadvertently reinforces messages about the importance of physical beauty. These revisions are wonderful books for girls to read and discuss, particularly when paired with readings of the original tales.

Retellings That Silence Female Characters

We do feel it necessary to note two well-known fairy tale revisions that do not counter the traditional role of the silent girl. These stories remain popular, suggesting how alarmingly attractive the silenced role remains for girls in our contemporary culture. The first is the story of "The Little Mermaid," originally penned by Hans Christian Andersen (1836/2002) and released by Walt Disney Pictures in 1989 as a full-length feature film (Musker & Clements, 1989). In this now well-known tale, a beautiful young mermaid falls in love with a human prince. To win his love, she gives her beautiful voice and her mermaid form to the Sea Witch in exchange for human legs. She is then unable to speak at all and must try to win the prince's love with only her beauty. This idea of forsaking voice for romance is dangerous. Moreover, the suggestion of literally sloughing off and reshaping unwanted body parts to please a man produces scary echoes of the extreme makeovers that young girls currently are seeing on prime-time television. Even more morbid, in the Andersen version, the mermaid experiences excruciating pain while walking on her newly acquired legs. In spite of the horrible pain she endures, the young mermaid in Andersen's story is unsuccessful in capturing the Prince's love, primarily because she cannot speak to him, and he marries another princess. However, in the Disney version, the mermaid Ariel is rewarded for her sacrifices by winning the prince of her dreams. These are both negative messages for young girls. We hope someone will recast this tale to show how two opposite young people can unite despite many obstacles without the girl character sacrificing everything that makes her unique.

Another tale that addresses a severe loss of voice is "The Six Swans" by the Brothers Grimm (Grimm & Grimm, 1977). This story is about a widowed lord who is tricked into marrying an evil sorceress. When the wicked bride finds out that her husband, suspicious of her magic, has hidden his seven children, she finds the lord's six young sons and turns them into swans. However, the lord's daughter escapes. She finds out that she can free her brothers from their enchantment if she does not speak for six years and sews six shirts out of starwort, a stinging nettle. The daughter is finally able to complete these tasks but at great cost: She is accused of murdering her own children and cannot defend herself. She is almost put to death on a burning pyre, but she manages to throw the shirts over her enchanted brothers just in time. This restores their human forms, and they save her.

A rewriting of the tale, *Daughter of the Forest* (Marillier, 2000), is set in ancient Ireland and contains elements about a political war with the Britons. Sorcha, the heroine of the tale, and her brothers become the victims of an ambitious, twisted stepmother. The enchantment and its antidote are the same: Sorcha must spend years in silence and in terrible pain, weaving shirts from starwort, to free her brothers. She is rewarded for this endeavor with love and happiness. Although it is a beautifully written and imagined romance, it perpetuates the idea that silencing oneself is a sacrifice a girl may have to make to ensure the happiness of the men in her life—and to ensure that her own romantic dreams are fulfilled.

Modern retellings of traditional fairy tales often revise the negative messages of the originals (competitive relationships with other women, rewards for female sacrifice and submission) into stories that celebrate female characters' agency and resourcefulness. The following discussion questions allow students to explore implicit messages in traditional fairy tales, as well as in retellings:

- In what ways are the girls' characters cast in passive roles instead of active ones? Why and how do they take charge of their own lives? What do they gain when they do? What are the consequences for not doing so?

- What sacrifices do girls make for others' happiness? How much do girls have a duty to make others happy versus how much they have a duty to make themselves happy? Would you make the sacrifices the girls do in these tales? Why or why not?

- In all these stories the girl ends up with a man, sometimes a prince, sometimes not. What makes these men the right ones for the girls to choose? Could not choosing a man also be a happy ending?

Women Warriors

Instead of rewriting popular fairy tales, many modern fantasy authors have written stories that replace the typical male hero of the quest story with female heroes. These stories advocate the idea of the woman as a warrior. The notion of training young women for combat is radical, even in the 21st century, when in most parts of the world women are still largely shielded from participation in direct military engagement. Therefore, it is exhilarating that a girl can read a fantasy novel in which the female protagonist is a battle commander. Most of these stories are written in series because elaborate fantasy worlds can rarely be explained in only one book. Two of the series that explore this theme are the Song of the Lioness series (Pierce, 1983, 1990, 2002) and the Damar stories (McKinley, 1982, 2000).

Female Warriors in Young Adult Literature

Pierce has used the European feudal tradition to re-envision the male quest story. In this system, young men were trained first as pages, then squires, then knights. In the first book of the Song of the Lioness series, *Alanna: The First Adventure* (1983), Alanna and her brother Thom are being sent away to school—Alanna to become a sorceress, Thom to become a knight. However, Thom has no wish to fight, wanting instead to study magic. Alanna, on the other hand, desires to be trained as a warrior. The children change places and Alanna, disguised as a boy, makes her way to the castle of King Roald, where she becomes a royal page. Alanna, using the alias Alan, distinguishes herself in both swordplay and loyalty. Alanna also discovers that she has the gift of magic. She becomes a favorite of Prince Jonathon, and together they defeat a mighty sorcerer. During their collaboration, Jonathon discovers that Alanna is really a girl but promises to keep her secret. The book ends with Alanna discovering that she has been chosen by the Goddess to become a mighty warrior. In the second book of the series, *In the Heart of the Goddess* (Pierce, 1990), Alanna becomes Jonathon's squire and his lover as well. In the third book, *The Woman Who Rides Like a Man* (Pierce, 2002), she passes the dreaded Ordeal and becomes a knight, finally revealing to all that she is a woman. She also rejects Jonathon's offer of marriage and queenship, instead allying herself with George, the King of Thieves. In the last book of the quartet, Alanna goes on a quest to find a magic gem and save the kingdom.

Using a more realistic approach for the Damar stories, Robin McKinley creates a setting similar to colonial India. At the beginning of the first book, *The Blue Sword* (1982), readers find out that the motherless heroine, Harry, has been raised without feminine influence; she prefers solitude and independence to society and artifice. When her father dies, she travels to live with her brother, who is stationed at a colonial outpost, Istan, near the tribal kingdom of Damar. Both Harry and the reader gradually become aware that the Damarian kingdom is home to magic and otherworldly beings. Corlath, the king of the Hillfolk, kidnaps Harry after he has a vision that shows Harry fighting valiantly for the Hillfolk during battle with their northern enemies. As a captive of the Hillfolk, Harry discovers that she has kelar, which gives her a mystical power of sight: She has visions of distant events, both present and future. Trained in horseback riding and sword fighting by one of Corlath's Riders, Harry becomes a skilled warrior and wins the horsemanship trials, defeating even Corlath. Later, ignoring Corlath's command, Harry leads her troops into a fierce battle against the demonic Northern Hordes, using magic as well as her skill in battle to defeat the invaders and save the Hillfolk. Rejecting the option of returning to the Homelander outposts, Harry chooses to stay in Damar. Corlath declares his love for her, and they marry. Harry's brother Richard and a few of the Outlander soldiers resolve to find a way for the two peoples to live side by side.

Both series raise fascinating questions about the nature of feminine power and agency. Alanna must disguise her femininity to become a warrior. Harry takes on a male aspect matched by her name, but only after being kidnapped: Her makeover is not initially her own choice, yet she excels in it. However, the androgynous nature of each character is extinguished in both series as they find mates. Alanna continues on as a knight. Harry, however, is engaged more in parenting than battle by the end of the novel, although this is also true of Corlath because they have brought peace to the kingdom. Both texts affirm the ability of women to function as both leaders and warriors. Questions that may help focus discussion on this topic could include the following:

- **To succeed in battle, why do the girls in these books have to hide their femininity and take on the role of males? Does this ever happen in our world? Give examples.**

- **Why might the author have chosen "Harry," a male name, for her female hero?**

- **Do you think these characters can, or should, continue their roles as warriors and guardians of the kingdoms after marriage and children, as men do? Why or why not?**

Dragon Tamers

Some of the most delightful voyages in fantasy are those books that involve dragons, which exist in one form or another in many cultures around the world (MacRae, 1998). Mythologically, the dragon is a symbol of what girls fear the most because these creatures are infamous for devouring young women, frequently princesses. Even more distressing, these young women are sometimes sent as sacrifices to a dragon to appease its ravenous hunger, thereby saving a town or village. In older tales it was the job of the warrior prince to slay the dragon, as illustrated in the story of Beowulf and the tale of St. George. Many fairy tales also require a young man to slay a dragon. After the feat is accomplished, the hero is often rewarded with the hand of a princess. The dragon, therefore, can symbolize for girls the fate of either being eaten or being thrust into an arranged future. However, what is interesting in modern YA fantasy literature is the number of books that cast girls in the role of *dragon-tamer* instead of dragon-slayer. Characters in this role use the nurturing quality typically associated with femininity as a strength in overcoming a fearsome beast. This wielding of feminine, rather than the traditionally masculine, form of power is found in three series, described in the following section.

Female Dragon Tamers in Young Adult Literature

The Enchanted Forest Chronicles series (Wrede, 1990, 1991, 2003a, 2003b) offers a humorous approach to the dragon tale. In the first book of the series, *Dealing with Dragons* (Wrede, 1990), Princess Cimorene runs away from her castle because she does not wish to be forcibly wed to Prince Therandil. She encounters a clan of dragons who debate whether they should eat her or just make her their captive. Desperate, Cimorene volunteers to be a servant to any of them with her skills in dancing, embroidery, Latin, and making cherries jubilee. Kazul, an important dragon, tells Cimorene that she can serve her. Cimorene becomes an integral part of the dragon world and learns magic. Happy in her new life, she rejects the offers of several knights who come to rescue her. Cimorene uncovers a plot by a group of wizards to overthrow the dragons, and when she foils the plot, Kazul becomes king of the dragons, a role that can be held by male or female dragons. The rest of the books in the series chronicle Cimorene's continuous adventures in the dragon caves.

Dragonsong (McCaffrey, 1976/2003) tells the story of Menolly, who lives in the fishing town of Half Circle Sea Hold. Her father and mother are perplexed by Menolly's desire to be a Harper (musician) because they think only males can become Harpers, so they ban her from making her own music. When she is burned in a kitchen accident, her parents purposefully allow the burn to heal improperly, hoping that Menolly will no longer be able to play the harp. Frustrated and desperate, Menolly runs away. She finds a cave, which is a hiding place not only for her but also for fire-lizards, a type of miniature dragon who adopt her as their mother. Isolated and alone and almost killed,

Menolly is rescued by a Dragon Rider. Once she is transported by the Rider to the Weyr where he lives, Menolly's musical talent is discovered and appreciated. In the sequel *Dragonsinger* (1977/1997), Menolly goes to Harper school, only to be met with animosity from the other female students, who are jealous of her talent and her control of the fire lizards. Nevertheless, she learns to value her gift and to work hard to succeed.

The Dragon Chronicles series begins with the novel *Dragon's Milk* (Fletcher, 1992), in which 15-year-old Kaeldra lives with her stepmother and her stepsister, Lyf. Kaeldra knows that she is different from the other Elythians; she is "farin" and descended from the Krags, a tall, blonde people who have unusual powers, which sets her apart from the small, dark Elythians. One of the Krags' powers is the ability to communicate with dragons. Kaeldra has inherited this power—she is a dragon-sayer, one who can sense the thoughts of dragons and speak with them. When Kaeldra's sister Lyf becomes desperately ill, the only possible cure is the milk of a mother dragon, so Kaeldra must travel to the hills where she has sensed a recent and rare dragon birth. Kaeldra becomes a mother for three orphaned draclings and succeeds in saving them and her sister as well. The final book in the series, *Sign of the Dove* (1999), tells the story of Kaeldra's stepsister Lyf, who, because she has drunk dragon's milk, now has the gift of dragon-saying, too. Like Kaeldra, she takes on the care and feeding of draclings and tries to get them to safety.

All three of these series explore the dilemma of a female character who does not fit the mold of expected behavior. Cimorene does not want to be a princess, Menolly desperately wants to be a Harper, and Kaeldra has an unusual gift that sets her apart from her adoptive family. Each of these young women is able to negotiate her differences and turn them into strengths. Part of this process involves taming fearsome, or at least rambunctious, dragons. These acts of nurturing and caretaking build strength in all the characters, allowing them to develop independence and capacity. The use of the traditional female role to develop strengths and talents is a great source of discussion about the powers of femininity. The following questions can help girls consider the underlying themes of these modern dragon stories:

- In traditional tales, the role of the male is to kill dragons. All of these girls, however, become "dragon sayers," rather than dragon slayers. What are the advantages of being a negotiator rather than a conqueror?
- All of these girls have difficulties fitting in. What is the relation between this difficulty and their relationship with dragons?
- What roles do male characters play in each novel, and how are these roles alike and different from traditional folk tale roles?
- What forces are at work in these stories to suppress the heroines' true voices? What actions do these heroines take to assert their true voices? What do they give up?

Magic Makers

Traditionally, women have been portrayed and perceived as the weaker, less powerful sex. Although this is clearly changing, many girls in the United States still feel constrained by prescriptive societal roles. Fantasy stories are especially empowering when they feature girls who have supernatural powers that make girls equal, if not superior, to their male peers. This equalization of power through supernatural gifts can be traced back to the end of the middle ages, when the stereotype of the female witch evolved (Bailey, 2002). Bailey suggests that witchcraft in the female was explained by uncontrolled sexuality. The female witch archetype flourished in Western literary tradition from Shakespeare's witches in *Macbeth* (2004) to the Wicked Witch of the West in Baum's *The Wizard of Oz* (1900/1993). Although fairy tales abound with females of supernatural power and also introduced the idea that a witch could be a benevolent as well as a malevolent character, witches generally have been feared, hated, and ostracized. However, in modern-day YA fantasy writing, girls can use supernatural powers for good instead of evil. Two recent fantasy series that confer extraordinary powers to girls who save their worlds are the Abhorsen series (Nix, 1995, 2001, 2004) and the His Dark Materials trilogy (Pullman, 2001, 2003a, 2003b).

Females With Magical Powers in Young Adult Literature

The first book of the Abhorsen series, *Sabriel* (Nix, 1995), introduces readers to a society similar to present-day Great Britain. However, there is a neighboring kingdom called the "Old Kingdom," which is separated from modern society by a wall and a perimeter. In the Old Kingdom, newer technologies do not function and magic prevails. The powerful force of the Charter, which is contained in special stones as well as in the bloodlines of the royal house and the Abhorsen line, works to provide energy for good. The Abhorsen family is gifted with the power to enter the kingdom of death and to bring dead humans back to life. At the beginning of the novel, Sabriel is graduating from Waverly, a boarding school, when she receives a strange visitor who sends her to the realm of death where she receives her father's sword and bells, the tools of the Abhorsens. Sabriel realizes that her father is dead and that he has turned over his powers to her. Desperate to rescue her father, Sabriel returns to the Old Kingdom and searches for his body, hoping to use her new powers to restore him to life. She is helped by a cat named Mogget and a handsome young man named Touchstone, whom she rescues from a spell. It soon becomes clear that the death of Sabriel's father is part of an evil plot to destroy the Charter. Sabriel must use all her skills to fight this evil and restore the Charter.

In the sequel *Lirael, Daughter of the Clayr* (Nix, 2001), which continues the story of Sabriel and Touchstone, we meet another remarkable young woman, Lirael, who lives in the caves of the Clayr in the Old Kingdom. The Clayr receive the gift of Sight early in life, allowing them to see the future, but by the age of 19 it is clear that Lirael is not to be endowed with this power. Miserable and friendless, she works in the library and teaches herself magic with the help of a magical creature called the Disreputable Dog. Unexpectedly, the Clayr have received a vision of Lirael confronting a sorcerer, so she travels to the Old Kingdom to make the vision come true. She discovers that she is the illegitimate daughter of the Abhorsen. She quickly learns the skills necessary for necromancy, and in this book and its sequel she becomes the Abhorsen-in-Waiting and helps Sabriel defeat the evil sorcerer.

Of all the powers imaginable, the ability to bring the dead to life is certainly the most awesome. Both Sabriel and Lirael are exceptional women who face the terrifying realm of death to protect others. They experience fear and loathing toward the dead, yet they overcome these feelings courageously. Although there are attractive male characters in these books, Sabriel and Lirael are strong females who earn the respect and fealty of their male peers. They eventually work with their male counterparts as equals. Sabriel and Touchstone's marriage is a remarkable partnership in which both exhibit power and nurturance.

In *The Golden Compass* (Pullman, 2001), the first book of the His Dark Materials trilogy, the reader meets young Lyra Belacqua. Since the death of her parents, Lyra has been raised by the scholars of Jordan College at Oxford University in England. However, readers quickly learn that things are not as familiar as they seem; the Oxford of the novel is in an alternate universe in which all humans are emotionally joined to magical animals, called daemons, which are their soul mates. Lyra learns that her parents are not dead but are powerful nobles who are committed to learning the secrets of traveling between universes. The secret to transversing the universes is to unleash great power, which can be done by severing the bond between a child and his or her daemon. Lyra's mother is conducting experiments in the northern lands to find a way to do this. She and her henchmen kidnap children to serve as fodder for these experiments. When Lyra realizes what is happening, she, along with powerful allies such as the Gyptians and the great armored bear Iorek, travels north to free the children from their prison. A key factor in Lyra's success is her singular ability to use a magical instrument called an alethiometer, which gives her the power to divine not only what is happening elsewhere in the present but also what may happen in the future.

Lyra is also a key figure in repairing the torn fabric of the universe, as is more fully explained in the sequels *The Subtle Knife* (Pullman, 2003a) and *The Amber Spyglass* (Pullman, 2003b). In these sequels, Lyra meets a young boy, Will, and together they fight the forces of evil and save the universe. Lyra and Will have a remarkable partnership in which both are completely equal to and respectful of one another. As Lyra uses the alethiometer, Will learns to wield a knife that can create entrances from one universe to another. Their love for one another is central to the healing force that repairs the world, but they also must sacrifice that love to complete the healing.

Both the Abhorsen and the His Dark Materials series postulate alternate worlds in which women have gifts that are equal to, and even sometimes surpass, those of their male counterparts. Women take on the heroes' roles in the classic quest tale structure, where they set forth on journeys to accomplish great tasks—Sabriel to rescue her father, and Lyra to save the children and, eventually, the universe. Their magical powers and tools become key to their quests by helping them to conquer many obstacles but do not prevent them from experiencing fear of failure or feeling isolation and loneliness. In fact, their powers seem to magnify their separateness. However, Sabriel and Lyra learn to use their gifts effectively, and in doing so they inspire the love and loyalty of others. The following questions can help students explore the magical qualities of these heroines:

- **The relationships of Sabriel and Touchstone and of Lyra and Will are both based on the principle of equal partnership between male and female peers. Can such a relationship only exist in fantasy worlds like these, or is it also possible in our world?**

- **How do the other male characters in these books influence Sabriel, Lirael, and Lyra? How does that compare to how other adult male–female relationships are defined in traditional tales or other books you have read?**

- **All the female protagonists possess extraordinary powers or tools. How do they choose to use them? Could they have accomplished their goals without supernatural powers?**

- **Discuss the physical descriptions of each character. Are they valued more for their beauty, intelligence, or strength? How do they use each attribute to their advantage?**

- **If you could have a supernatural power, what would it be, and how would you make the most of it?**

Female Deities and Sisterhood

Some YA fantasy novels have borrowed from South American, Celtic, and Greek mythology to create worlds in which women rely on one another in all-female societies or worship a female deity. These stories counter the male patriarchy of much of Western European culture. Muten (2003) identified over 100 goddesses, many from the Western tradition, celebrated with stories of strength, wisdom, and kindness. Most Western readers are familiar with the Greek goddess Athena (Roman name, Minerva), who was the goddess of war, but also preferred using her wisdom to avoid bloodshed through negotiation. Another famous goddess is the Greek Demeter, who was responsible for the fertility of the crops. When Demeter's daughter Persephone was abducted, Demeter withheld her gifts of bounty until the gods relented and had Persephone returned. The Egyptian goddess Isis was a compassionate ruler who served her people as physician and teacher. These incredibly strong figures often inspired cults of worship and young women who dedicated their lives in the service of the goddess.

Goodrich (1990) has documented many of the histories and myths of all-female societies such as the Amazons, warrior women who fought on horseback; the moon priestesses of Crete; the Furies; the Priestesses at Delphi; and the Vestal Virgins of Rome. Goodrich explains that these priestess orders included women who served as healers, mystics, lecturers and/or prophets. Many of the priestesses descended from noble families; their numbers sometimes climbed to the thousands. Often the role was passed from mother to daughter. They inspired awe and admiration from both men and women in their culture due to their perceived gifts of prophecy, purity, and sacrifice. These strong female figures and communities are imitated and restored in some YA fantasy literature.

Goddess and Sisterhood Stories in Young Adult Literature

In the books of the Great Alta Saga (see, for instance, Yolen, 2003a, 2003b), a world similar to Anglo-Saxon England is revealed. Alta is a mother-goddess, and the women who worship her live in all-female communities called Hames, which are led by a Mother Alta. The women in the Hames take on various occupations, and many become warriors. Women who grow up in Hames are able through magic to call forth a spiritual twin, or "dark sister," after they reach puberty. This dark sister is an alter-ego who provides constant companionship. In the first book of the series, *Sister Light, Sister Dark* (Yolen, 2003a), the protagonist, Jenna, becomes a warrior. As is the ritual for all followers of Alta, she leaves the Hame of her birth on a trek to visit other Hames. On her way, she meets Prince Carum, who is trying to escape death at the hands of his evil uncles. Jenna fights one of the uncles and kills him, and then she takes Carum to a large Hame to hide him. The surviving uncles find Carum, destroying the Hame and all its defenders. Jenna escapes the slaughter and discovers that she is really the rebirth of the mother goddess, Alta, and that it is her duty to defend the sisterhood.

Books in the Daughters of the Moon series (see, for instance, Ewing, 2000a, 2000b, 2001a, 2001b) provide a modern setting, unlike many fantasy stories that features girls. The first book, *Goddess of the Night* (Ewing, 2000a), tells the story of four Los Angeles high school girls, each of whom has special gifts: Vanessa can disappear; Catty can travel through time; Serena can read minds; Jimena can foresee the future. The girls gradually meet one another and realize that they have a common bond—they all wear a moon amulet that glows when one of the other girls is nearby. They finally meet a retired history teacher, Maggie Craven, who explains that they are all moon goddesses. When they reach the age of 16, they must choose either to give up their gifts and live a normal life, or disappear into an unknown world where they can remain goddesses. Meanwhile, their task on earth is to fight the power of evil, which exists in an organization known as the Atrox. What is significant about these books is that the girls protect and nurture one another. Of course, there are also "bad girls" who are part of the evil Atrox, but the books focus on the relationships among the four goddesses. The girls' closeness is made even more remarkable by their diversity: Jimena comes from a background of poverty and violence, while Vanessa is from a nuclear, middle-class family, and Catty was adopted by a spiritualist. Despite their differences, the girls are committed to one another, and even their romantic relationships take a backseat to this strong bond.

The notion of a an all-female community, where girls support one another and take on all leadership roles, is compelling. We see elements of this on college campuses with girls' involvement in and devotion to their sororities and their sorority sisters. Girls are not used to having a space where they are not competing for male attention and where they can share wisdom and strength, so such female communities are important. The goddess and sisterhood aspects in these books can be examined with the aid of the following questions:

- **What are the differences between good and bad girls in these stories? What is the appeal of each?**

- **In what ways do the girls you know support one another? How could they (and you) do more to protect and nourish one another?**

- **What aspects of the female characters in these books are traditionally male traits?**

- **What would be positive and negative about growing up in an all-female (or all-male, if you're a boy) society?**

- **What women are role models in U.S. society? Whom do you admire, and why? Why do you think there has never been a female president in the United States, when other countries like Great Britain, Panama, and Israel have had female leaders?**

Vampires and Werewolves

One of the current trends in fantasy for young adults, particularly girls, revolves around the legends of vampires and werewolves, which have in common the idea of a monster that preys on helpless victims, often female. Despite the horror and danger of these monsters, they often are attractive to their female victims. The vampire offers immortality through feeding off human hosts; the werewolf combines both the danger of the predator and the lure of sexual gratification. This attraction-repulsion causes young people to question whether they want to break taboos and explore the unusual, the strange, the grotesque, and the forbidden. Several popular YA authors make use of supernatural creatures, offering girls an opportunity to explore the lure of the dark side.

Confronting Dark Creatures in Young Adult Literature

Companions of the Night (Velde, 1995) begins when 16-year-old Kerry does a favor for her young brother and returns to a laundromat to retrieve his stuffed animal. In the laundromat, she saves an attractive young man from what appear to be kidnappers. However, after the rescue, she learns that the young man is a vampire, and the kidnappers were vampire hunters. The vampire, Ethan, convinces Kerry to help him escape his captors. During their flight, Kerry begins to fall in love with Ethan. She must make a choice: Allow Ethan to make her into a vampire and join his world, or reject him and remain human. Clearly this book demonstrates girls' fascination with the forbidden, but it suggests that it is necessary to reject the forbidden to remain human. The book also suggests that submission to what is forbidden results in unhappiness because Ethan has lost most of his family and friends over the long course of his undead state.

In *Blood and Chocolate* (Klause, 1997), attraction to the supernatural wins out. The protagonist of the novel is Vivian Gandillion, a beautiful 16-year-old girl who happens to be a werewolf. Like the rest of her pack, Vivian cannot control the change that happens to her during a full moon. Although it is discouraged, Vivian develops a relationship with a young "meatboy," or human. Gentle, handsome Adrian is enamored with the idea of werewolves, but when Vivian reveals herself as one he panics and rejects her. Instead of wallowing in sorrow, Vivian chooses to mate with her pack's leader and celebrate her uniqueness. This book encourages girls to see themselves as strong and fearless, and to resist the urge to see themselves as ugly when others do so.

Along with many others like them, these books allow girls to explore the meaning of normalcy, the price of difference, and the attraction and repulsion both of the taboo and of feelings that are forbidden. The novels allow girls to consider the tendency human beings have to define groups of people they see as different as less human than themselves, often as a way of justifying the social power they have. The vampires and werewolves of these novels are marginalized groups; this is a source of both fear and attraction for the humans with whom they come into contact. This concept, and its relationship to girls' development, can be explored with the following questions:

- **What is the attraction of predatory monsters like vampires and werewolves for girls? For boys?**
- **Why do some characters in these books ultimately prefer normality, while some deliberately choose to be part of the marginalized, ostracized groups?**
- **Are there girls you know who have joined groups that are ostracized? What are they like? How are they treated?**

Women in Science Fiction

Although many writers consider Mary Shelley's *Frankenstein* (1818/2004) to be one of the first works of science fiction, the genre has typically been the province of male authors and male protagonists. Early modern science fiction authors include famous names such as Isaac Asimov, Ray Bradbury, and Frank Herbert. Their stories almost universally portrayed space exploration or colonization led—often exclusively—by males. This, no doubt, was due to the pairing of science fiction and space exploration, which was expected to have a militaristic structure—and in the United States, women were not allowed in the front lines of battle until recently (albeit in drastically limited ways). Early science fiction written for adults was devoured by teenagers, again mostly male, so the need for YA science fiction has not been as acute as the need for YA contemporary fiction or even YA historical fiction. Although movies such as *Alien* (Carroll, Giler, Hill, & Scott, 1979) and *The Terminator* (Daly, Gibson, Hurd, & Cameron, 1984) began to feature female protagonists, introducing prototypes for the strong, savvy fighters of the future, YA science fiction's characters and readership remain primarily male. Some notable exceptions exist, however, and they beautifully coincide with the theme of this book by portraying girls in search of authentic voice and establishing themselves as strong and capable.

Female Characters in Young Adult Science Fiction

Keeper of the Isis Light (Hughes, 2000) won the 2000 Phoenix Award, an honor presented by the Children's Literature Association that recognizes books that were published 20 years previously but were not widely appreciated at that time. Orphaned early in life, this book's heroine, 16-year-old Olwen Pendennis, has been raised alone on the planet Isis by a kindly caretaker simply called Guardian. Her life changes when a ship with 80 colonists arrives on Isis and she befriends Mark, an attractive boy her age, sharing with him the beauties of her planet. However, when Olwen removes the protective clothing and mask that Guardian insists that she wear, Mark recoils in horror. Olwen is not outwardly human. Unbeknownst to her, Guardian has genetically adapted her to life on Isis by turning her into a reptilian creature. Mortified by her physical differences from the colonists, Olwen refuses to have anything to do with them. After she heroically saves a child from danger the colonists offer to restore her body to its original form, but Olwen refuses, deciding instead to move further away from the colony and live alone with Guardian. Olwen rejects her prior need to become like the colonists and returns to her happy state of companionship and freedom.

This story is remarkable for its stance that it may be preferable for a girl to live without a romantic or sexual partner, rather than conform to societal expectations. It especially challenges traditional physical beauty and lookism, as reflected by the answer Guardian gives Olwen when she asks him, "Am I ugly?" He replies, "No! You are not ugly at all. Form and function should be as one. You function perfectly. You are beautiful" (p. 111). Olwen comes to revel in her differences from the colonists, rather than seek to eradicate them.

Unlike Hughes's novel, *A Wrinkle in Time* (L'Engle, 1962) received acclaim from the time it was published, winning the Newbery Medal. In this story, teenage Meg and her younger brother Charles Wallace are dismayed when their father disappears. They travel through the universe on a desperate quest to rescue him, aided by three "wise women" who have magical powers. Meg is a misfit in her high school, a nerd who is skilled in mathematics, but as she travels through space she grows more self-confident. Interestingly, her main character flaws—anger, stubbornness, and impatience—are encouraged by the three wise women, and these traits become strengths rather than short-comings. This is an important point of discussion with girls because these traits are so often discouraged in them, yet accepted in boys. In the novel, Meg is able to use her strengths to help find her father and protect her brother.

Both of these books set strong female characters in futuristic settings and challenge traditional ideals of female traits. Curiously, far fewer women write science fiction than write fantasy. Perhaps this is because fantasy novels often pattern themselves after fairy tales that offer more traditionally female roles, and it has been difficult for authors to stray from the typical science fiction pattern of male roles. As more women enter scientific fields and read what little science fiction has been written by women, we hope the trend will change. Questions that can help girls examine these books include the following:

- **How do these science fiction novels with girl protagonists showcase their problem-solving abilities?**
- **What is the effect of the authors' choice to create female characters who do not fit the traditional definitions of beauty, but who prove to have a lot of internal strength and power?**
- **Both Olwen and Meg find a clear voice with which to speak against those who want them to conform. What allows these girls to find their voices at the ends of their respective novels?**
- **How do adults and/or peers help girls find their true voices?**

Summary

Fantasy and science fiction novels offer visions of worlds other than the one we know. Therefore, they offer girls an opportunity to think in new and different ways about female choices and roles. It is fascinating to discuss these alternatives and compare them to the dilemmas that girls face in their own lives. Many of these stories contain metaphors for choices that girls make daily, such as whether to go out with "bad boys," whether to do well in mathematics and brave the label of "geek," and whether to reveal their innermost selves to people they love—and how to respond to the possible rejection. This comparison to real life allows for exciting discussions about the outcomes of those choices and their possible benefits and pitfalls.

A teacher who wishes to introduce science fiction or fantasy to adolescent girls can focus the discussion solely on a character in a fantasy book, allowing students to distance themselves from the analysis if they choose, yet inviting them to make comparisons to their own circumstances. By using the framework in Figure 1 (see page 23) as a tool, students can clearly see the forces at work in shaping a protagonist's voice. As students read more and more about strong girls who face numerous obstacles, they will be able to internalize the ideas. The lesson that begins on page 140 allows students to be creative in responding to a humorous work of fantasy.

SAMPLE LESSON PLAN

Lesson Topic
Writing from different perspectives

Lesson Objectives

- Students will effectively analyze the points of view of different characters in a novel.
- Students will write collaboratively, creating a single product.
- Students will use a written voice appropriate to characters from the novel.

Instructional Materials
Class set of novel *Dealing with Dragons* (Wrede, 1990); poster board for each group; magic markers

Activities and Procedures

Day 1: Introduce the Text (5 minutes)
Read the first chapter aloud, and then assign students to read chapters 2 and 3. Students should then get into groups of four to discuss the following questions.

Discussion of *Dealing with Dragons*—Guiding Questions (10 minutes)

1. What did you think of Cimorene? Does she remind you of anyone you know?

2. How is Cimorene different from other princesses that you know about? Why do you think the author chose to make Cimorene so different?

3. How does Cimorene try to express herself? What does she want to be or do? Are your goals or hopes similar to hers or different? Why?

Creative Writing (15 minutes)
Assign each group to become one of the following characters: Cimorene's father; Prince Therandil; Woraug; Kazul; Alianora; and one

of Cimorene's sisters. Ask students to consider the following question as if they were the character: What would you advise Cimorene to do at this point in the story, if you were one of the characters in the book? Would you advise her to go home, to stick it out, or to run away?

Each group is to write their advice to Cimorene based on their interpretation of how the character in the book would respond. Assign reading the next section of the book, chapters 4 and 5, as homework.

Day 2: Response to Writing (15 minutes for sharing advice; 10 minutes for discussion)
Take the part of Cimorene, and ask each group to read their advice to you as if you were Cimorene. Then discuss as a class the different pieces of advice and which advice Cimorene should follow.

Use the framework from Figure 1 (see page 23) to guide students through further discussion of the following questions:

1. How is Cimorene expected to behave and act in her society? What is expected of you?

2. How do Cimorene's parents help or try to stop her from being herself? Do your parents ever do this? How and why?

3. How do other prince and princesses help or try to stop Cimorene?

4. How do the dragons help or try to stop Cimorene? What other adults help you? How?

For the rest of the class, and then for homework, ask students to read the next section, chapters 6 through 9.

Day 3: Discussion and Creative Writing (10 minutes for discussion; 20 minutes for writing; 15 minutes for sharing)
Lead students in discussion of the following questions from their reading:

1. How does Cimorene change as the story develops? What causes her to change?

2. How much control does Cimorene have over her choices? When does she seem to have the most control?

3. Does Cimorene care a lot about her looks? Why or why not?

Ask students to group-write a diary entry as if they are the character they used in day 1's writing assignment. This diary entry is to reflect the character's thoughts on Cimorene and her antics. The entry should indicate whether the character approves or disapproves of Cimorene's actions and why.

When writing time is over, groups share their diary entries. Assign for homework reading the remaining chapters of the book.

Day 4: Closing Activities (25 minutes total for discussion; 20 minutes for writing)

Lead the groups in discussing the following questions:

1. What surprised you about the way the story ended?

2. How is Cimorene's fate different than that of Alianora? Why did the author make this happen?

3. What is ironic about Kazul becoming king of the dragons?

4. What will Cimorene's next adventure be? Why do you think so?

Have each group lead the discussion on one question.

For the final activity, direct each group to write a positive or negative proclamation about Cimorene that would be issued by the character from whose perspective they have been writing. (First you may have to explain that the point of a proclamation is to make a public announcement that celebrates or condemns a person's actions. You may want to give examples from well-known stories such as "Beauty and the Beast.") The groups' proclamations then will be written elegantly with magic markers on poster board. Students should share and post their final proclamations.

Evaluation

Assess students on their group assignment writing, specifically assessing whether the writing correctly incorporates story elements, authentically appropriates the voice of the character, and has one coherent voice.

CHAPTER 6

Discussing the Books: The Extracurricular Girls' Book Club

OW THAT we have made a case for leading girls to read about and discuss their developmental issues, and identified different genres and individual books that support good discussions, we can consider simple ways to create environments that support productive and open discussions. This chapter and chapter 7 consider two such environments for discussion: (1) extracurricular book clubs and (2) in-class group literature study. These are certainly not the only two discussion vehicles you could use; with the rapid development of technology and students' comfort using technology, online forums and chat rooms are other great ways to open and sustain conversations about books. However, book clubs and in-class group study represent easy and effective ways to expose all students to these great books, in and out of the classroom.

The key element of a book club, as we define it, is that it is completely voluntary: Students choose to come to a place where they can discuss books they are reading. A second feature is that all book club members read the same books at the same time so their discussion can have a narrower focus. And finally, book clubs offer flexibility of schedule: Students can meet at lunch time, on Saturdays, or during the summer.

History of Book Clubs

Book clubs have a colorful and interesting history, and have had a close affiliation with women's development of voice. Book clubs came into existence shortly after books began to be widely distributed, in part for social reasons—book discussions gathered people together—

and in part for economic reasons—books were expensive, so a group of people could buy several books and share them. Some of the earliest known book clubs were organized in Paris during the 1600s and 1700s. These gatherings were called *salons* and were often held by hostesses who were writers themselves (Adams, n.d.). Important figures in politics, literature, and art were invited to discuss new works.

Anne Hutchison, a Puritan religious leader, is often described as the founder of the first book/study club in (colonial) America (Laskin & Hughes, 1995). In 1634, she organized groups of women who met twice a week to discuss the Sunday sermon. Unfortunately, this came to the attention of the male clergy. The club was disbanded, and Anne was banished from the Massachusetts Bay Colony. From that point on, female literary clubs in early America, if they existed, took care to keep a low profile.

In the early 1800s, "reading parties" began to emerge in Boston (Laskin & Hughes, 1995, p. 3), often attracting young women who were not welcome in collegiate settings. Guest lecturers would address *bluestockings*, a derisive term during that era for a group of intellectual woman, who would then discuss the lecture. In 1877 women in the small town of Mattoon, Illinois founded perhaps the earliest community book club (Hooper, 2001). Members, all female, took turns hosting meetings in their living rooms. This served as a model for what most people think of as the traditional book club. It was replicated in many towns across the nation, and many of these book clubs still exist today.

In the late 1800s, several women's club were established, most notably in Boston and New York, to discuss literature. The women who participated in these clubs were largely upper class. Some men supported their efforts, but others complained that the club members should "perform some useful task like knitting socks" (Laskin & Hughes, 1995, p. 5). Nevertheless, the clubs persisted. Generally, they met for several hours during week days because women were not supposed to go out after dark.

The Great Books Foundation was established in 1947, providing housewives a chance to read and discuss books identified as important in Western culture (Laskin & Hughes, 1995). Within its first year of operation, Great Books had more than 43,000 members in 300 different cities (Adams, n.d.). Great Books continued to flourish throughout the 1950s and 1960s but then began to be replaced by more popular types of reading materials, which were sponsored by clubs in libraries, schools, churches, and homes.

Talk show host Oprah Winfrey has been credited for revitalizing book clubs by establishing Oprah's Book Club in 1996 (Adams, n.d.). Many of the books she selected are written by women, or have women as their primary audience. This phenomenon has been studied by Long (2003), who spent years profiling the book clubs meeting during the mid-1990s in Houston, Texas, and found that 60% of the book clubs meeting there were women only, 30–35% were a mix or men and women, and 5–10% were men only. Long attributes this phenomena to human desire to socialize in an environment in which one can freely discuss all kinds of issues. It is fascinating, however, that so many book clubs have been dominated by women. This certainly lends credence to the notion that women generally are considered more verbal than men, more interested in reading novels, and more comfortable sharing their feelings.

Book Clubs in Schools

With the renewed attention on community book clubs, it is not surprising that school teachers, librarians, and reading specialists have begun instituting book clubs in schools. One of the most publicized efforts is that of Chicago's public schools, in which Mayor Richard M. Daley initiated book clubs in 1998 after he served as Principal for a Day at Orr Community High School on Chicago's West Side (Mayor Daley's Elementary Book Club, 2003, para 2). The mayor participates in some of the book club discussions, and noted authors such as Stephen King and Scott Turow have been invited to discuss their works. Because of the program's success, book clubs also have been implemented in some of Chicago's elementary schools.

A great addition to the book club at Inglemoor High School, Washington, is the club's website, which posts book reviews written by club members (Inglemoor High School Library Book Club, n.d.). A review of *I Was a Teenage Fairy* (Block, 2000) includes the following comments:

As usual, Francesa Lia Block's beautifully unique style held my attention on its own, but this sad story is not to be forgotten. The title refers to how Barbie's mother pressures her into becoming a reluctant fashion model, but it also carries a deeper meaning. This is a story for any girl who has ever been unsure of herself. (Inglemoor High School Library Book Club, n.d., p. 3)

The Inglemoor club meets most Tuesdays during a scheduled clubs period. The club hosts speakers at its meetings, and members go on field trips to author signings.

In Tidewater, Virginia, a librarian and a reading specialist at a middle school host a lunchtime book club for students in which they bring whatever they are reading and talk about it. They meet every other Friday during lunch. Students are allowed to bring their lunches into the library. There are six sessions, which run consecutively, since there are six different lunch periods; attendance varies from four students to over a dozen. All students are welcome as long as they are willing to talk about reading.

Students have even instigated school book clubs on their own. Shortly after the opening of Highlands Middle School in Cincinnati, Ohio, students asked their librarian if they could begin a book club based on Oprah's Book Club (Croyle, 2003). The book club has been in existence ever since.

Some book clubs are held in the summer months to make use of students' break from homework. Kelly Chandler reported a wonderful example of a summer book club in the *Journal of Adolescent & Adult Literacy* (1997). Chandler issued a written invitation to her tenth- and eleventh-grade English classes:

Do you want to improve your mind, have an intensely fun experience, and get to spend quality time with me this summer? If your answer is "Yes! Absolutely" to all three of these questions, you will want to join the book group I am trying to form. I'd like to see if we can read four books over the summer and meet four times to hang out and talk about them. There is a strong possibility that we may also go on some adventurous field trips if people are enthusiastic.

The books I'm thinking about are fun, interesting, and challenging—but probably not ones you will read in class. Meetings will be very informal, combining scintillating discussion, deep thinking, and relaxed banter (a tall order, but I think we're capable of it). You do not have to come. You do not have to read all the books. You will most assuredly not be tested on them! (p. 2)

Chandler (1997) had 17 students join the book club that summer, 37 the next summer, and 24 the third summer, and both Chandler and her students deemed the experience successful. Chandler discovered that certain elements benefited the students. First, the opportunity for open dialogue caused more students to express their ideas. Second, articulating their ideas in a supportive environment caused the students to become more confident in their reading and comprehension of texts. Third, Chandler found that the book club influenced her teaching strategies. She became much more willing to express her ideas as tentative hypotheses for the group to consider, rather than trying to lead students to her ideas about the text. She also assigned much more responsibility to students, such as allowing them to lead discussions, because she gained more faith in their abilities to do so.

Book Clubs for Girls

For teachers and other adults concerned about girls' development of authentic voices, a book club for girls can provide a forum for dealing with issues that are otherwise difficult to address. Broughton (2002) describes the ways in which discussing literature can assist girls as they construct their identities in late childhood and adolescence. Broughton points out that the understanding of one's identity is "constituted through discourse and practice and is continually constructed and reconstructed" (p.3). The discussion of literature, then, allows this construction to happen in two ways: First, literature provides vicarious experiences that can substitute for practice; and second, in group discussion, girls can articulate their thoughts, revise them, and respond to the thoughts of others.

A reader encounters a text and responds aesthetically, with enjoyment, but also with empathy and identification with the characters. The initial response to a book evolves from a sense of self and identity. For example, 13-year-old Karen, reading *Shabanu: Daughter of the Wind* (Staples, 2000) for the first time, might respond to the book in a discussion group with a spontaneous reflection on the horrors of arranged marriage. In doing so, she is practicing vicariously what she would feel and do if she were living that experience. During a discussion of the book, she might hear another girl mention that although Shabanu really did not seem to mind the prospect of an arranged marriage to Murad, who was young and handsome, she dreaded the idea of an arranged marriage to Rahim-sahib, who was old and already had three wives. This might lead to a general discussion of what creates happiness in a marriage and what type of husband would be best. Another girl might wonder aloud if women really need to get married, or if women like the novel's Aunt Sharma are really in the best situation because they are totally independent and do not have to worry about pleasing a husband. Through hearing other responses and having the time to articulate her thoughts, Karen will begin to construct ideas about what men provide in a marriage and what she is willing to do and not do in order to create a marriage partnership.

Teacher Michele Haiken explains, "Book clubs provide opportunities for girls to speak out about their feelings and experiences as they relate to the stories discussed. Through characters' eyes and their own reflections, girls become aware that they are not alone" (2002, p. 411). After watching her seventh-grade girls silence themselves in her classroom, Haiken created a girls' book club that provided "a set place and time to share their voices and be heard" (p. 411). Her female students began to meet for 90-minute sessions each week. Haiken argued that the girls-only meetings helped girls to do the following:

1. Raise consciousness and socialize in a safe environment

2. Gain self-knowledge and self-esteem

3. Enhance communication and

4. Realize the power that they possess over the direction of their own lives. (p. 412)

A number of research studies involving girls-only book clubs have been reported in the literature regarding the subject. Carico (1996) set up a book club as part of a research study to determine the effects of using a reader response approach to literature with middle school girls. Generally, reader response approaches acknowledge that each reader brings a different set of experiences to the text and thus will interpret it in a highly personal and individual way (Nodelman & Reimer, 2003). Carico selected *Roll of Thunder, Hear My Cry* (Taylor, 1976/1991) and *Lyddie* (Paterson, 1991) as the books for discussion. Carico met with four middle school girls 15 times over a period of four months. She had the girls discuss the characters in the books, how they did or did not identify with them, and how they approached reading the novels. She found that the girls used the books to discuss many issues: "sexism, racism, romance, religion, their homes, and their perceived personal faults" (p. 212). The reader response method allowed the girls to explore their own feelings and analyze the ways in which the books' characters dealt with challenges. Carico encountered some problems in the book club, including the occasional use of inappropriate language, negative comments that girls made about teachers and other students in the school, and times that the girls wanted to discuss other books or nonrelated issues. Nevertheless, Carico felt that the book club affirmed that literature "evoked strong emotional responses and provided the means for cognitive and emotional growth" (p. 225). The girls reported that the conditions of the group made it easier for them to talk openly: "It was small; there were no boys; I [the researcher] was an outsider" (p. 231).

Other book clubs for girls have been established specifically to examine girls' issues. Irwin-DeVitis and Benjamin (1995) organized a summer book club for girls ages 11 through 13. Nine girls from four different schools volunteered to attend the club, which met during the evenings. The girls read only one book: *Anne Frank: The Diary of a Young Girl* (Frank, 1953). Irwin-DeVitis and Benjamin selected this book because of its frequent use in schools; however, they felt that it was more commonly used to study a historical account of the Holocaust than to explore girls' issues. Irwin-DeVitis and Benjamin wanted to examine the issues of voice and relationship explored in the writings of Brown and Gilligan (1992), so they centered discussions around what society expects from girls. One question asked was, which is more important for girls: looks or brains? According to the authors, the girls were very aware of the pressure that society placed on them to be "nice" and "submissive and silent," which conflicted with the girls' desire to be "strong, courageous and outspoken" (p. 14).

The girls identified with the character of Anne Frank and bemoaned the fact that she was pressured to act more like Margot, her passive, compliant sister. The authors concluded that

> educators have an important role in encouraging girls to confront the dilemma of maintaining voice in relationships and helping them to question societal expectations to be pretty, passive and compliant.... Vibrant literature depicting strong female adolescents is one avenue through which such discussions can begin, and the healthy development of all our adolescents, male and female, can be fostered. (p. 15)

Smith (1997, 2001) also constructed a book club for girls as part of a research study. Smith and eight sixth-grade girls at a northeastern middle school met for 17 sessions over a period of six months. The girls, generally good students and readers, participated in the selection of four books: (1) *The Beggar's Ride* (Nelson, 1992/1994), (2) *I Hadn't Meant to Tell You This* (Woodson, 1995), (3) *The Friends* (Guy, 1973/1992), and (4) *Phoenix Rising* (Hesse, 1995). Smith purposely selected novels with strong female characters to encourage student responses to positive portrayals of girls in literature. The club met once a week for an hour, during which time students discussed the readings and wrote letters to the characters in the novels. Smith videotaped the meetings and interviewed girls individually at four points during the study. Smith found that the girls definitely were able to identify with the protagonists in the novels, and the girls were able to vicariously experience negative situations, such as the abuse experienced by Clare in *The Beggar's Ride*, and negotiate these negative experiences through discussion. Smith admitted her unease in dealing with some of the issues raised in the books, such as rape and "child pimps," but reflected, "I recognized the importance of a safe, intimate forum for early adolescent girls to explore these issues together" (2001, p. 12). She concluded that the girls' book club was a way to structure experiences for girls that allowed them to understand the challenges and dangers of the world around them, and it offered them ways to negotiate these challenges (Smith, 2001, p. 12).

A wonderfully intriguing book club called the Go Girls Book Club has been established by Grace Diggs, a Boston Public Schools teacher. Following a field trip to the Boston Women's Memorial, Diggs and her high school girl students decided to establish a book club "concentrating on stories of young women who deal with personal and social challenges" (para. 1). The girls, including some below-average readers, meet weekly to discuss books. Peer leaders select titles, and members record their reactions to the books in journals. The club strives to increase awareness of good books; the girls "share ideas with the school community through book talks, newsletter reviews, and library exhibits" (para. 1). At the schoolwide Service Learning Festival, members of the club discuss the pleasures of reading to girls from neighboring schools. In addition, the girls plan to invite prominent women in their community to talk about the involvement of women in community activities.

These examples are excellent models and inspiration for the many types of book clubs that can be created and the many ways in which they can function. However, there are basic guidelines for teachers, media specialists, or others who would like to set up book clubs at their school. These are developed below.

Setting Up a Book Club

A number of excellent books can help adults establish a book club, including *The New York Public Library Guide to Reading Groups* (Saal, 1995) and *The Reading Group Book* (Laskin & Hughes, 1995). Most of these books are written for adult clubs, so they set different parameters than may be appropriate for adolescents' clubs, but the key tasks outlined are the same for book clubs for any age group. We have taken the major elements and adapted them to a school book club, offering options that we and others have tested.

Who Should Run the Club?

Unlike adult book clubs, where hosts may rotate among members, school book clubs need adult sponsors. Even in high schools, where students often assume the role of discussion leader, an adult sponsor should be present for legal reasons, as is true for all extracurricular activities. Extracurricular book clubs can be sponsored by a teacher (often an English teacher feels most comfortable leading discussions of literature), a reading specialist, a media specialist, a counselor, or another adult, such as a university researcher or a parent. If the club's host is not employed by the school, however, it is important to have a school-based cosponsor. When we ran our after-school book club, an eighth-grade English teacher agreed to be a cosponsor. She allowed us to meet in her classroom, and she was present during most of the meetings, but she did not take a leadership role. She also was invaluable in helping recruit students into the club.

Having two leaders may be optimal. According to Saal (1995), the Great Books Foundation program requires the presence of two co-leaders. One is tasked with moving the discussion along without giving his or her opinion, while the other makes sure that everyone in the group participates. We observed this process at a book club meeting at a local middle school, and it was very effective. However, not every school has the luxury of having two staff members able to give their time and energy to a book club.

The role of the sponsor or leader is critical in the school setting. He or she must be warm and encouraging, interested, and willing to listen. In many cases, the leader will guide the discussion, and he or she must get the club members to participate. "The New York Public Library measures a successful book discussion by how *much* the group talks and how *little* the leader talks," writes Saal (1995, p. 42).

Who Can Join the Book Club?

Because school book clubs are voluntary, everyone who wants to join can probably do so, but there are some conditions that might limit membership. First of all, if the group is a book club for girls, then it should be limited to girls only. This is a tough call to make because both boys and girls benefit from discussing girls' issues. However, girls have expressed that they appreciate time and space to talk about their own special concerns. Research conducted on six middle schools, reported in the AAUW 1996 publication *Girls in the Middle* (Cohen & Blanc, 1996), found that the most common program that supported girls was an all-girl group, often led by counselors or teachers, that allowed discussion of girls' issues. The authors concluded,

> At least on a short-term basis, girls' groups appear to encourage girls to develop autonomy with the help of supportive adults and are places where girls can address and even argue through their differences. As one girl explained, "We can say what we want. We don't have to worry about what the boys will say." (p. 82)

Because middle and high school students are undergoing puberty, there will always be some romantic and sexual tensions in mixed-gender settings. (Apparently this does not change in adult book groups, some of which have been used as singles' clubs.) When we ran our group at the middle school, we simply advertised it as a book club for girls, so no boys applied.

Another limitation on membership might be the size of the group. Almost everyone writing about book clubs agrees that they should be limited to 20 members, and most prefer groups of 10 or 12. Interestingly, many find that when they limit the number of students in a group to 20, over time only about 8 to 12 become "regulars." In our group, 18 initial applicants signed up, but only 9 came to the first meeting, and attendance usually ranged from 6 to 8. In our observations of groups larger than 12, it appeared difficult to get everyone involved, and there were often sidebar conversations that detracted from the group discussion.

When and Where Should the Book Club Be Held?

Student book clubs require less time than adult book clubs, which often run for two hours. The most successful middle school student discussions are often an hour or less, while high school students are able to hold longer meetings. For this reason, school book clubs can easily meet in a classroom or in the school library. Again, school book clubs can meet after school, at lunch, before school, on Saturdays, or even during the summers. Each has its own advantages and disadvantages. We do not know of any before-school clubs because many students arrive at school just before it starts. Meeting after school can work because most schools have extracurricular activity transportation for students who do not live near the school. It is also fairly easy to find space and time to meet after school. However, many activities, especially athletics, meet at that time; we lost some of our best book club members to sports practices.

Lunchtime offers another possible meeting slot, as it presents less potential conflict with other activities. One local school created a "Brown Bag and Book Club" in which students brought their lunch and a book, discussing while they ate. A principal at a local school noted how enjoyable it was to enter the school library at lunchtime and see a group of students eating their lunch and enjoying talking about books. However, many schools do not have one lunch period but multiple periods, thus fracturing a single group and requiring more than one meeting time. This might be an obstacle for a teacher who only has one lunch period available for meetings but should be doable for media specialists. Another problem is that often the lunch periods are short, and by the time students arrive and unpack their lunches, there is less than half an hour left for discussion.

Most adult book clubs meet once a month, which gives members plenty of time to read a single book and allows them to schedule a fixed time to meet, such as the first Wednesday of every month at 7:00 p.m. Student book clubs can follow this format, as well, but meeting every two weeks provides a sense of continuity and allows for the many school holidays that might otherwise interfere with meetings (i.e., Thanksgiving, winter recess, spring break, etc.). One teacher we met ran a high school book club for girls that met every two weeks, but it became so popular she started another club that met on alternate weeks. She felt that this was optimal for the continued participation of her female members.

Summer book clubs are obviously less constrained than those meeting during the school year; the students can meet every few weeks or more often. However, summer vacations and camps can create attendance problems for some students. Another possible obstacle is the lack of a place to meet because school buildings are sometimes closed in the summer.

How to Advertise Your Book Club

Once a sponsor has decided on the logistics of a book club, he or she can advertise it using flyers, announcements on the school intercom, postings on the school website, or personal invitations distributed to students in English classes or homerooms. Our book club benefited from personal letters we distributed to all eighth-grade girls. Once a book club is up and running, word of mouth may attract new members, which is important because some original members likely will be unwilling or unable to continue coming.

If the club plans to read and discuss controversial books, participants' parents should be asked to sign a permission form that lists proposed books or discusses the purpose of the club and provides a general overview of the types of books that will be discussed. Parental permission is particularly important for clubs in elementary and middle schools. We sent home permission forms for our book club and felt that it really forestalled any potential concerns of parents; further, none of our club members' parents refused to sign the permission form.

Selecting and Acquiring Books

There are several different thoughts on book selection for book clubs. In general, the more input members have in the selection, the more interested they will be in coming to the meetings. In a school setting, there are many constraints upon book selection because not all students have the means to purchase any book that the club votes on. In addition, because the club is focused on girls' issues, there are certain books that are more appropriate than others.

In our book club, we identified a list of books and let the girls select which one they wanted to read first, and after we completed that book, we had students vote on what to read next. We listed more books than we had time to read, which allowed some choice, and we provided books for all the girls. We felt that providing books would prevent an initial loss of members who could not afford to buy a book or whose parents did not have time to drive them to a bookstore.

The earlier chapters in this book have provided an easy guide to possible book selections that can benefit girls' development. One way to identify potential books from which your book club chooses is to find out what class sets the school has. Class sets are a cheap and easy way to provide books to every club member. Media specialists often have a budget for purchasing class sets, so interested sponsors can submit lists of books they think will be useful in book clubs. At our middle school, the media specialist took us to a large room where class sets of at least 30 books were stored.

Some active book club websites suggest raising money to buy books by putting together car washes, bake sales, and used book sales. Leaders can also order used books online for low prices and keep these books as class sets for future clubs. Sponsors such as the PTA and local chapters of state reading associations also may support the purchase of books. Our book club project received a grant from our university to purchase the books we needed through the university bookstore, and then we donated the books to the school with which we worked.

Keep in mind, not every book club member will like all the books selected for discussion, but what does not work for one group may be appreciated by another. For example, one book club sponsor we met said that after discussing *The True Confessions of Charlotte Doyle* (Avi, 1992) her high schools girls begged her, "No more of those corset books!" In contrast, our diverse group of middle school girls really enjoyed the novel. Rather than give books away after a bad reaction, it is better to save the sets and try them later.

What to Do at Book Club Meetings

The main purpose of a book club is to discuss the book, which of course requires students to have read it. At the first meeting, then, leaders explain a general outline of reading expectations. The most successful book clubs appear to be those that discuss one book per meeting and expect all their members to have read it before the meeting. For avid readers, this is not a problem—two weeks is plenty of time to read a book for pleasure. In a study of one adolescent book club, the members read voluntarily for "an average of 46 minutes a day, seven days a week, over a fifteen week period" (Alvermann, Young, & Green, 1997, p. 13). This meant that the club members were reading approximately 10.5 hours per week, or 21 hours in two weeks, which is a far greater amount of time than most students would need to finish one book. Of course, most adolescents do not spend this much time engaged in voluntary reading; a 2003 study conducted by the U.S. Bureau of Labor showed that teens spend an average of only seven minutes a day reading paper-based material, not including homework (Johnson, 2005). Realistically, though, the students who join book clubs are the ones who like to read.

Many authors have offered helpful suggestions about how to have good book club discussions. Alvermann, Young, and Green's 1997 study offers a fascinating insight: Students in the book club "were forthright in their declarations that the [book club] discussions should not resemble classroom discussions" (p. 13). The students saw their typical classroom discussions of literature as "structured and boring" (p. 13), and they seemed to appreciate a more free-wheeling, personal approach to discussion. This atmosphere encourages personalized response, which also seems to be the best way to explore girls' issues.

The New York Public Library Guide to Reading Groups (Saal, 1995) suggests simple guidelines that, if followed, will foster good discussion: "speak up; listen thoughtfully to others; be brief; and come with questions in mind" (p. 32). Leaders can set these guidelines at the club's first meeting or can use them as a model for students who wish to create their own guidelines. The key to good discussion seems to lie in the quality of the questions asked by the facilitator and the willingness of members to openly share their ideas. *The New York Public Library Guide* adopts the tenets of the Great Books program in advising its leaders to

> Ask questions that initiate, sustain, and try to conclude investigations into problems or issues found in the book.
>
> Ask questions that challenge all unclear, factually incorrect, or contradictory statements.
>
> Classify all responses according to your best judgment. Select those statements you want to question immediately; ignore those you find uninteresting, trivial, or irrelevant; and table those you may want to question later. (p. 35)

The most important duty of the girls' book club leader is to devise questions that investigate the problems that girls face as they maneuver through adolescence. The framework established in chapter 2 (see page 23) suggests a series of questions to spark important discussion:

- Who are the girls in this story? How do they express their voices? What do they say and do, and does this change during the book?

- Is each girl able to express her own voice? Why or why not?
- Does the girl experience support or constraints from female and male peers? In what way(s)?
- Do the girl's parents support her authentic voice or try to quell it? How about other adults?
- How do societal expectations influence the female characters?
- Does the girl experience "lookism" or focus her energy on her physical appearance? In what way?

The questions from this framework should provide critical insight into some of the major issues confronting girls. Repeating these questions with each book discussion will encourage girls to compare female characters within a book and also between books.

There are many additional questions that can spark good discussion, as well, and *The New York Public Library Guide* (Saal, 1995) suggests that these questions be used to initiate discussion:

- What is the book about? Talk about the ideas, not the plot.
- To you, what are the important themes?
- Is this a book driven primarily by plot, by an idea, or by its characters?
- What are the main characters' distinguishing traits? What do you admire or dislike about them?
- Describe the interaction among the major characters. What are the most important relationships in the book?
- What are the most revealing scenes? Do they further the action of the novel?
- Are any of the events depicted relevant to your own life? (p. 43)

This last question holds the most promise for helping girls to connect literary experiences to their own. Girls sometimes cannot connect their own lives to these issues because they have minimal experience, but as stated previously, experiencing events vicariously through literature also can provide a type of interaction that allows girls to think through and solve problems that they may encounter someday.

Laskin and Hughes (1995) suggest additional questions that might be interesting to pose in girls' book clubs, including the following:

- What do you think the title means?
- Why do you think the author opened the book this way?
- What other books that the group has read could you compare this one to?
- Did the jacket copy give you a fair idea of what the book would be like?
- Why has the author chosen this particular narrator? Can you imagine this story told in a different voice?
- Did this book make you want to read anything else by the same author? (p. 77)

One of the most difficult challenges in leading girls through a series of thought-provoking questions is allowing them time to think. A New York Public Library book club leader wrote,

> One of the most important things that I learned in working with reading groups is how to keep the discussion going along.... What is hard is to allow some silence. At first, I kept wanting to fill in with a question about the book. It took me a while to be able to allow a little silence, which gives people a chance to think an idea through and then express themselves. You get some of the most thoughtful observations that way. (Klucevsek, cited in Saal, 1995, p. 34)

Although discussion is the most fruitful aspect of book clubs, leaders can plan other activities to keep students interested. This is especially important for young students or older students whose schedules force longer meeting times. (It's hard to discuss a book with 12-year-olds for longer than 45 minutes.) Some recommended activities are discussed below (Mayor Daley's Elementary Book Club, 2003).

Draw, write, and find other ways to respond to the book. Teachers have long had access to lists of ways that students can respond to texts. One of our favorites is "75 Ways to Share a Book" (Barchers, 1988, p. 19), which offers numerous activities that students can do after reading a book. Some specific activities include making a map of where the story takes place, making up a limerick or haiku about the book, making a timeline of its events, rewriting one of its incidents for a younger reader, role playing one of the characters, writing a few pages in a diary as if you were one of the characters, or planning the questions you would use in a conference call interview with the author.

Students often like to write book reviews. Many schools now have webpages that advertise and explain their book clubs, and student reviews can be posted there. Library bulletin boards are another venue to post book reviews. Writing and posting a book review gives book club participants the feeling of being published, strengthening the sense of kinship they feel toward the authors of the books they read. A sample book review from the Inglemoor High School Book Club's webpage is included earlier in this chapter.

Watch videos or listen to audiotapes of books. Even our college students ask us if they can watch video clips from some of the stories they read. Although the nature of the book club is literary, it is fascinating to watch videos after reading a book to compare our vision of the novel's characters and setting with someone else's. It provides a way to spark discussion about interpretation. Video performances can also highlight key ideas. For instance, the most recent film version of *Little Women* (DiNovi, Swicord, Carr, Armstrong, & Lewis, 1994) highlights the close relationship between the girls and their mother; it also focuses on Jo March's attempts to voice her authentic self. Audiotapes are also powerful, as has been demonstrated by the wonderful audio performances of the Harry Potter books. Having a professional actor read parts of a novel is also exciting because he or she often uncovers nuances that have been missed by readers.

Invite guest speakers. Because the number of published, professional writers is small, most young people never get a chance to hear about how books are written and published. It is exciting for book club members to have a published author come to talk to them about his or her approach to writing—how ideas emerge, how the author allocates space and time for writing, and what the process of finding a publisher is like. School-based book clubs cannot usually attract well-known authors, but published authors live in almost every city and often are featured in the daily newspaper. Every Sunday, our newspaper prints a segment featuring local authors; a recent edition featured a travel book about Greece and a collection of poems by a retired archeologist. Local authors are usually happy to speak at school book clubs.

Author programs are also available through subscription at some web services; TeachingBooks.net provides online interviews with authors of many YA books. BookClubs.ca offers clubs the chance to facilitate a meeting with an author, though the site features primarily authors of adult books. Another idea is for students to become "biographers" and write articles about their favorite authors through the site LITWEB.net.

Librarians are also effective guest speakers. The Inglemoor High School Book Club invited a local librarian to talk at its club meeting ("Book Club," n.d.). She spoke about her personal favorite YA books and a library program called "Read 3 Get 1 Free." She also gave book talks on several books, including books by authors Jane Yolen, Donna Jo Napoli, and Charles De Lint. Public librarians can introduce students to new authors and genres, as well as convey their excitement about new literature.

Conduct field trips. Newspapers are good sources of information about events that feature authors and books, such as author signings, book talks, and readings hosted by local bookstores and libraries. For instance, a recent Sunday paper announced a poetry reading by writers from a local university at an art gallery on Sunday afternoon, a book discussion of *To Kill a Mockingbird* (Lee, 1960/1988) at the local public library on Tuesday evening, and discussions of film versions of books and graphic novels on Tuesday and Thursday nights at a local Barnes & Noble bookstore. Any of these events would make an interesting field trip. Of course, because book clubs are voluntary, any field trips should be voluntary as well. Still, it is important to work within school guidelines concerning transportation and liability issues.

Maintaining Attendance at Club Meetings

There are two generally agreed-upon tips for keeping attendance high at book clubs: (1) Give students effective reminders, and (2) provide food. If the book club only meets once a month, or even once every two weeks, students are apt to forget about the meeting time. There are several ways to remind members. One way is to utilize school announcements because meetings are usually during the school day. Reminders a few days before a meeting make it more likely that students will have read the book before attending the discussion. Another tactic is a "phone tree," in which the sponsor calls two people, who in turn are assigned to call two people, and so on until everyone has been reminded. This is a nice way to encourage interaction between book club members, and it invites early discussion about books. In schools where nearly every member has access to e-mail, an e-mail reminder can easily be sent out by a member designated for that task. A free Web resource that assists in organizing and sending reminders for Book Club meetings is www.generousbooks.com, which offers to send e-mail reminders as well as assist sponsors in finding books and guest speakers for club meetings. Another idea is to use the site www.Evite.com to send free electronic invitations and reminders to attend club meetings.

Most authors writing about book clubs agree that food is a delectable and helpful addition to a book club. Laskin and Hughes (1995) note, "a reading group...binds a group of readers together in personal as well as intellectual ways. So why not enjoy feeding the body as well as the soul?" (pp. 86–87). Some suggest that if a meal is planned, it should be served prior to the discussion. Of course, in most school settings it is unlikely that a meal will be served, but in the book clubs we have observed, sponsors usually provide some type of snack or dessert. Members can also alternate the task of bringing a snack for everyone, with a reserve in place in case someone forgets. Members can bring snacks that would be found in the setting of the book; for example, a student might bring pita bread and hummus when members are reading *Habibi* (Nye, 1999), a novel about a U.S. girl who moves to Palestine. Another method, described earlier in this chapter, is to have book club meetings at lunch and ask that students simply bring their lunch with them to eat. (This can cause a bit of a conflict, however, if students forget their lunches and then have to wait for a cafeteria meal purchase.)

Predictable Problems and Possible Solutions

One of the most prevalent problems of book clubs, both those for adults and for young people, is that members sometimes attend without having read the book or having read only part of it. This can lead to disinterest in the discussion and members who do not want others to "give away the ending." The website www.teenreads.com (2004) recommends that groups decide for themselves what to do about this problem at the very beginning. For instance, a rule for the club could be that members should attend only if they have read the book, or that if they have not finished they must be prepared for discussions about the whole book.

Another issue to prepare for is the tendency of members to engage in off-task conversation. A local middle school media specialist stated,

> With the larger groups, there are a lot of side conversations that start that have nothing to do with books. With the older kids who know each other, there is a lot of interrupting of each other, and a lot of talk about things other than books. (personal communication, June 26, 2004)

This website also recognizes that a main challenge is to

> keep the discussion focused on what you're reading and not how hot Sally looked today or Chris's new sneakers. If a Reading Club turns into a Gossip Club, it won't last long, but if it sticks to books, it'll be a big success. (2004, para. 11)

Our observations of book clubs showed that a skilled facilitator is the key to keeping students on task. Redirecting members to the book at hand, then asking specific questions about the text, seems to refocus a group on appropriate discussion. Also, a small group size seems to diminish this problem.

Summary

Book clubs are an excellent way to engage students in the kinds of discussions that foster examination of girls' development. Book clubs are voluntary, so they usually attract students who are already committed to literature and are eager to engage in discussions. Girls' book clubs can be organized in a variety of formats and can be facilitated by any teacher or media specialist. Fortunately, many guides have been written about how to run effective book clubs, and there are wonderful examples of school book clubs to draw from. Using the Internet is helpful both in starting a book club and in getting more ideas about which books to select and what activities to offer. Although there are potential problems with maintaining a book club, they are well worth the effort. Both girls and boys can benefit from facilitated discussions of the issues girls face as they are posited in good literature.

CHAPTER 7

Using the Books: In-Class Activities

LTHOUGH SCHOOL book clubs are highly attractive to students because they offer an intellectual environment free of the restrictions of assignments and grades, a large number of students will not participate. They may be too busy, disinterested in reading, or think book clubs are only for "brains" or "nerds." If discussions of girls' issues are truly to be made part of a school's agenda, they should be systematically built into the curriculum. This is what the authors of *Girls in the Middle: Working to Succeed in School* (Cohen & Blanc, 1996) recognize in their advice on addressing issues of gender in a school setting. The authors suggest that schools should "make gender visible" (p. 69). Specifically, they describe a desirable outcome as "re-form...connected to girls' and boys' adolescent experiences and developmental needs—both distinctive and shared" (p. 88). They recommend that teachers do the following:

> Open dialogue on gender issues in the classroom. Discuss gender as an aspect of students' lives, curricular materials and classroom dynamics. Don't restrict the discussion to classes such as Family and Consumer Sciences, which deals explicitly with female and male roles, but encourage them whenever the curriculum or classroom interactions warrant. Gender issues are often tied to cultural issues. Use curricula and materials that show females and males from various cultures in a variety of roles. (p. 88)

This type of dialogue is ideally suited for the language arts classroom, in which teachers are required to have students read and discuss fiction and nonfiction that is often selected because it relates to young people. Teachers should choose fiction that they know will generate good discussions of girls' (and boys') issues. There are several ways in which teachers can incorporate catalyst texts into the classroom; the whole-class novel and literature circle approaches are probably the simplest to put into practice. This chapter discusses each of these approaches and gives specific examples from classrooms in which they have been used.

The Whole-Class Novel Approach

To use the whole-class novel approach, the teacher should assign one novel that everyone reads. There are a number of advantages to this approach. The most important of these is that all students react to the same text, so students can consider important points about how gender is handled in the book more easily. This is appealing to many teachers, especially when it is their first time grappling with an important theme. A second advantage to the whole-class novel approach is that most school libraries and English departments have class sets of books that have already been purchased, making it easy to identify books to use.

Most school districts identify literature appropriate for each grade level, which prevents teachers from accidentally teaching the same books to students in different grades. Many of these books lend themselves well to discussions of gender issues, and many of these books match ones we have identified. (Interestingly, many novels on recommended reading lists contain girls who must deal with issues of both gender and ethnicity.)

Thanks to reading lists, books that have been preapproved can be assigned, and teachers do not have to worry about raising parental concerns or not fulfilling district curriculum expectations. Each book on the reading list has been identified as having literary value, and the gender issues addressed by these books make valid discussion points.

The whole-class novel approach should begin with an introductory activity before or during distribution of the novel. A prereading question will activate students' prior knowledge. For example, when presenting *Farewell to Manzanar: A True Story of Japanese American Experience During and After the World War II Internment* (Houston & Houston, 1983), one could ask students, What happened to Japanese people who lived in the United States when World War II started? A novel unit on *Flipped* (Van Draanen, 2001) could begin with the question, Are there kids in your neighborhood who are very different from you? Students can write responses to these questions, while the teacher allows them quiet time to consider their answers; the teacher also should make sure that each student has something to contribute. The whole-class discussion that follows this activity engages students in sharing personal experiences that relate to the book's topic. The goal of this prewriting exercise, then, is to reveal experiences and opinions, not to correct wrong impressions.

Another type of introductory activity is a prediction question, which is often asked while the books are distributed. Students can look at the cover of the book, and perhaps the chapter titles, and then predict what will happen in the book. The teacher can create an interesting variation of this activity by writing key words or phrases from the book on the board and asking students to project what the book will be about. For instance, a list from *Fever: 1793* (Anderson, 2002) might include the words and phrases *Yellow Fever, death stench, coffee house, Free African Society, Philadelphia, 1793, Mattie (age 14), mercury and calomel, Grandfather ill, painter Mr. Peale, picking berries*. Students working in small groups then try to weave the words together into a story outline by sharing their ideas. Both activating and predicting activities are helpful in getting students motivated to read and ensuring that they will better comprehend the text when they begin reading. In addition, the teacher might read aloud the first part of the book (perhaps the first chapter) before assigning independent reading.

After the introductory activity, students' readings should be assigned based on the chapter divisions of the book. Typically, students will read the chapters to be discussed in class for homework and spend several weeks on the novel. To hold students accountable for their reading, the teacher can give a brief quiz on the assigned chapter (containing just a few questions with obvious answers, not obscure, miniscule details that frustrate struggling readers). Or students can keep a log of their responses to the material. Grading these activities helps motivate students to read the assigned text. During the class period, frequent minilessons should be taught on elements of the novel, such as plot, theme, characters, imagery, conflict, or historical factors.

What is most difficult about the whole-class novel approach is engaging all students in discussion. Typically, only 10–20% of the class will choose to answer the discussion questions posed. The remainder of the class will choose to sit apathetically and listen. To overcome this difficulty, many teachers put students into small work groups (clusters of 3–5 students seem to work best) to discuss questions. The groups should have 10–20 minutes to collaboratively answer these questions. Then, after the small groups have completed their discussions, the teacher should invite responses from the entire class. This makes students much more willing to respond because they are more confident of their ideas, having clarified them by sharing with other students first. Often the backmatter of a novel contains questions for discussion, and there are many websites prepared by teachers and targeted to the various texts that offer other provocative questions. Of course, the questions provided throughout this book will get students thinking about gender issues, as well.

Using the Whole-Class Novel Approach to Discuss Voice

Paul Lawrence is a high school teacher who uses whole-class novels that provoke interesting discussion. Paul has organized his curriculum to include "LitTalk Day," a once-a-week occurrence during which students discuss the adolescent literature that they are reading independently. Paul introduces a novel to his tenth-grade students in week one. This year, the novel selected was *Speak* (Anderson, 2003). Paul instructs students to read the first quarter of the novel at home (it breaks easily into fourths because it is organized around the nine-week grading periods used in most high schools), and he gives students a week to read that portion of the novel.

When students enter class on LitTalk Day, to ensure they have read their assigned chapter, they first take a quiz that tests basic knowledge of the characters and events in the novel. Paul collects their quizzes and briefly goes over the answers; then he asks students to respond in writing to several prompts that require them to think more deeply about the novel. For instance, after the first quarter of the book, students respond to these questions:

1. What is Melinda's home life like? What kind of support does she get from her parents? Do you think her home life is believable? How important is parent support for success?

2. What is Melinda's peer group like? Does she fit in? Why or why not?

3. What is Melinda's voice? Who is she and what does she believe?

4. Have you ever experienced anything like Melinda does in this high school or other schools?

Students write quietly for about 10 minutes on these questions. This writing time is critical because it allows time for students to contemplate the questions. Writing about discussion questions also helps those who are reluctant or reticent about sharing in group discussion because they will have prepared their thoughts ahead of time.

Once the writing time expires, Paul asks the students to move their desks into a circle and bring their writing with them. Students must follow the following rules:

1. Students are to use a "talking ball" to control the discussion. This small, lightweight ball is held by the person speaking. When he or she is finished talking, another student indicates that he or she wants to speak, and the ball is thrown to the new speaker.

2. Everyone listens respectfully to the person speaking.

3. The teacher is a listener, recording who talks and briefly noting interesting points.

4. Students who contribute two or more thoughtful and pertinent comments receive 100 points for a quiz equivalent. Students who contribute one such comment get an 88 (B); students who listen respectfully but do not contribute get a 79 (C-).

5. Students may discuss their written responses to the questions, or they may discuss other things in the text that they have read.

Paul sits on the outside of the circle as students begin to discuss Melinda's home life. The talk is interesting and lively. Many students participate, and the ball moves back and forth among the 30 pupils. Paul stops the discussion after about 10 minutes to summarize some of the interesting points that have been made and to suggest that the students move on to the topic of Melinda's school life. The discussion resumes. At the end of another 10 minutes, about half of the students have contributed something to the discussion. Paul now asks the students to pass the ball around the circle. Students who do not wish to speak can simply pass the ball along; however, this gives everyone one last chance to contribute to the discussion. This strategy results in almost every student contributing a comment. Paul summarizes the main points of the discussion and asks the students to read the next section of the book by the following week.

Paul modifies this practice for students who are reluctant readers; he allows class time for reading, especially when he is given a double-period language arts block. This encourages students to read. But the key to success, Paul believes, is finding literature to which his high school students can relate. If a book is interesting to them, they will read it and talk about what they have read. Paul tries to keep independent reading fun and low-pressure; no major papers, tests, or projects accompany these books. Those assignments are saved for assessing the rest of the curriculum, which Paul teaches during the remainder of the week. After observing his high school classes, we can attest to the effectiveness of Paul's approach.

Student Reactions to the Book

In Paul's classroom, students have strong reactions to reading the novel *Speak*. The girls confirm that their high school is in many ways like Melinda's, though not quite as stratified. They agree wholeheartedly that they want to fit into at least one group, though many claim to have membership in several "clans." The girls especially talk about how important it is to have friends. The boys agree, though they seem less passionate in their responses. Students are surprisingly frank when they respond to questions about Melinda's home life. Many talk about how close they are with their parents, and how much they rely on their parents for emotional support. Others describe very strained relations with parents; one girl admits, "My father and I don't get along at all." All the students agree that Melinda's parents are not living up to their responsibilities.

One of the questions that teachers typically ask, especially male teachers, is how to lead class discussions about sensitive issues such as rape or pregnancy. Paul says,

> I try and create a safe environment...I let the students do most of the talking. Of course, I monitor what they say, and don't let the discussion get off track or allow anything that is hurtful to be said. But overall, the kids are pretty respectful of one another. I think the key is getting a good book and letting students start to care about the characters. When my students read *Imani, All Mine* (Porter, 2000) and we get to what is a pretty graphic rape scene, the students really care about Tasha, and they want to talk about what happens to her. They are attached to her as a person. It's a powerful tool to open up student discussion. (P. Lawrence, personal communication, April 27, 2006)

Another important issue that may be encountered by teachers who lead literature discussions around young adult issues is what to do when students become emotionally distraught over the content of what is being discussed. For instance, at the university level, we have had girls in tears; others have come to us before or after class to say they cannot stay because the novel being discussed is too close to what has happened to them. (This especially is true when we teach novels that deal with rape.) It is important to offer to connect students to counselors in these instances because it is critical that girls (and boys) have access to professional help beyond that of literature discussions. Because every secondary school has a counseling staff, it would be important to discuss referral processes with counselors prior to beginning any discussions of sensitive topics to determine how to proceed if students reveal real psychological problems.

Literature Circles

Whole-class discussions are difficult for some students. Adolescents may be too embarrassed to offer their opinions in front of 25 or more of their peers, especially when sensitive topics are discussed (and sometimes teachers are uncomfortable as well). Using literature circles may address this problem. Literature circles are small groups that meet to discuss books that students are reading. According to Daniels's (2002) helpful resource on literature circles, these groups have three main characteristics: First, they offer students some choice; second, they encourage diversity of outlooks; and third, they force students to assume responsibility for their work.

In general, to make a literature circle work a teacher should select a theme to be studied and choose texts to match. According to Raphael and colleagues (2001), there should be some introductory study that is completed with the whole class. Raphael's book gives specific, lengthy examples of how this might play out in a classroom. For instance, when studying a unit on civil rights, students could read about the subject and write a research paper on aspects of the Civil Rights movement. During this time, the teacher could also read aloud from works such as *Rosa Parks: My Story* (Parks, 1999), the true story of a black woman who refused to give up her seat on a bus to a white person. Students could also read or listen to the audiotape of President John F. Kennedy's Radio and Television Report to the American People on Civil Rights (1963), in which he addressed the integration of schools in Alabama. The class could then be introduced to four different novels that focus on civil rights: (1) *I Know Why the Caged Bird Sings* (Angelou, 1970/1983); (2) *The Watsons Go to Birmingham—1963* (Curtis, 1995); (3) *To Kill a Mockingbird* (Lee, 1960/1988); and (4) *Roll of Thunder, Hear My Cry* (Taylor, 1976/1991). Students would select which book they wanted to read and create small groups responsible for discussing the work.

Peer-led literature circle discussions are the heart of the experience. Students should have a set time limit for reading their group's entire book. For example, Daniels (2002) writes of a fifth-grade teacher who gives three weeks for the class to complete reading a book. He suggests that in a middle school setting, students should meet in groups for 45 minutes on alternating days, using the nonmeeting days to read and work on reading assignments. If the luxury of class time is not available for reading, the reading assignment should be homework. A high school plan suggested by Daniels proposes that students meet every other day for a week and then only on Fridays until reading is concluded. Students are responsible for setting up a reading schedule that will fit the classroom framework, and the teacher should approve the reading schedule. During times that the class is not meeting in literature circles, the teacher can work on minilessons that support the theme of the unit or specific literary analysis skills.

Self-directed student discussion is crucial to the literature circle but is also the most difficult aspect. Daniels (2002) recommends and gives copious examples of roles that can be assumed by students to facilitate discussion. For example, a discussion director guides student discussion; a connector helps students connect what they read to their own experiences; an illustrator provides a graphic representation of something in the text; a literary luminary selects passages to be read by the group, either orally or silently. Daniels writes that these "task descriptions are designed to support genuine *collaborative learning* by giving kids clearly defined, interlocking jobs to do" (p. 60). Students arrive at their groups prepared to provide what their roles demand, so they have very specific things to share. Obviously, this greatly aids in the efficient use of group time. It also offers teachers written products that can be collected for assessment purposes. Other roles that Daniels suggests are vocabulary enricher, travel tracer, summarizer, and investigator. Roles should be rotated each time the group meets, to ensure that students have opportunities to examine different aspects of the text and that no one is inadvertently silenced due to a particular role.

Other scholars have suggested different ways to foster good discussions. McMahon and Raphael (1997) recommend that students write response logs and think-sheets before coming to literature circle discussions. For instance, students can write questions for the author, produce a character map, or create a sequence chart that includes literary elements they are studying in the regular curriculum. These activities provide more flexible forms of reader response to guide discussion.

Generally authors agree that literature circles should have between four and eight members (Brabham & Villaume, 2000; Farinacci, 1998) because larger groups make it difficult for everyone to contribute. Also, groups should be as heterogeneous as possible. McMahon and Raphael (1997) talk about the need for students to see one another as contributing readers and writers, regardless of their backgrounds. Students also can learn from one another's experiences. The teacher is an important figure in the process because he or she can model how books can be discussed and provide input to groups that are struggling. The teacher also should provide input on "multiple literary elements such as plot, characterization, setting, point of view, tone and symbolism" (McMahon & Raphael, 1997, p. 61).

One important component of literature circles is the opportunity to reflect on how they are operating. McMahon has prepared a "Stepping Back" survey, which asks group members to reflect on questions such as, "Did I read the assigned pages?" "Did I write in my log book before starting Book Club?" "Did I write any questions for my group?" and so on (p. 105). Self-assessment is a powerful way to help groups develop.

Another critical part of the literature circle is the groups' presentations of what they have learned or accomplished. Daniels (2002) refers to the class time during which students share their insights as the *sharing session*. Not only is this a way to force students to synthesize what they have learned from their literature discussions, but it is also a way to recruit other students to read different books. Some of the ways that to share books include the following:

- Posters advertising the book.
- Readers Theatre performances.
- Reader-on-the street interviews (live or videotaped).
- An artwork—painting, sculpture, poem, mobile, collage, diorama—interpreting the book.
- An original skit based on the book.
- Diorama of the book. (Daniels, 2002, pp. 68–69)

Raphael, Kehus, and Damphousse (2001) suggest extending a themed unit after the shared presentations of books. For example, in the unit on civil rights discussed previously, the teacher could read aloud the children's book *Song of the Trees* (Taylor, 1975) and have students respond to it. Also, students could listen to Martin Luther King, Jr.'s "I Have a Dream" speech (1963) and respond. Students could study contemporary civil rights issues and discuss how they are being addressed. These activities allow students to apply some of the concepts they have encountered in their literature circles.

All implementers of literature circles agree that it takes time and energy to guide students to successfully use this strategy. Daniels

(2002) points out that when he first tried this model, "the kids didn't always have the social skills that they needed to function in peer-led discussions" (p. 48). Daniels began to teach students the skills of group discussion prior to implementing the strategy. Students practiced these skills by reading and discussing small pieces of fiction or nonfiction, starting with five-minute group interactions—first in pairs, then in groups of three, then in clusters of four or five. Daniels emphasizes the value of well-written short stories in familiarizing students with the literature circle model.

Raphael and colleagues (2001) provide an extensive list of themes that appeal to adolescent readers, including conformity, divorce, heritage, immigration, risk, and sibling rivalry. Several themes are of particular interest because they relate to girls' issues: gender, male and female viewpoints, and women's rights. Johnson (2000), a middle school educator, focused her literature circles on girls' issues, choosing to use girls-only groups because she thought girls were more likely to talk freely if boys were not present. She reports that her hypothesis was accurate: Girls in girls-only literature circles were more likely to critically address gender issues and to recognize stereotypes in the literature than those in mixed groups.

Using Literature Circles to Discuss Voice

We tested focusing literature circles on a girls' issues in collaboration with a classroom teacher, Lori Risher (Sprague & Risher, 2002). Lori had always taught a fantasy unit as part of her seventh-grade literature study, and because so many early adolescents, both boys and girls, are fascinated by fantasy literature, we decided this genre would be an excellent vehicle for generating classroom discussion about gender issues. From the books we recommended in an earlier publication, "A Library for Ophelia" (Sprague & Keeling, 2000), we selected four as fitting the genre of fantasy: (1) *Ella Enchanted* (Levine, 1998); (2) *Dragonsong* (McCaffrey, 1976/2003); (3) *Dragonsinger* (McCaffrey, 1977/1997); and (4) *Dealing with Dragons* (Wrede, 1990).

Each of the books was chosen based on three major criteria. First, the main character of each novel was female. This greatly limited our choices because many fantasy books have male central characters. Some of the works with male protagonists might have been suitable, but we felt that our goal of addressing girls' issues would be met more effectively using a book with a female protagonist. Second, in each book the main character struggled against societal expectations that attempted to limit her personal goals and ambitions. Third, the main character was successful in achieving her authentic voice—she fulfilled her ambitions by demonstrating strength, which included self-awareness (recognizing both her gifts and her weaknesses); willingness to confront parents, peers, and outside forces; and determination, as evidenced by her continued struggle against these forces. (See chapter 5 for a more thorough discussion of plot and themes for each of these titles.)

Lori decided to teach the books in all four of her language arts classes, which ranged in size from 22 to 26 students. Because this was a research project, we sent letters explaining the purpose of the unit to all parents and asked for written permission allowing students to participate. (Only 1 parent out of almost 100 refused to give consent.) Lori formed the class into groups of five to six students based on reading level because the books provided a range of reading difficulty.

Each group was tasked with reading one book over a two-week period. Groups developed their own timelines for reading the book, and Lori arranged small-group and whole-group discussions, and led minilessons. To guide students' reading response, Lori also assigned a daily diary, which consisted of journal entries that students recorded after reading each chapter. Students had to write from a first-person point of view as though they were a character in the novel. They also had to develop a question and find one interesting vocabulary word in the chapter to share with their group. This formed the basis for their small-group discussion.

The 10 class days were organized as follows:

Day 1: Lori introduced the books and explained the fantasy genre. She also explained that these books contained a similar theme, which students would discover through their reading. Students met in their groups, were given the books, and completed prediction charts based on a cursory inspection of the book's title, cover, and book jacket. Students set timelines for reading the book. Lori explained the daily diary assignment.

Day 2: Lori conducted a minilesson on setting, paying particular attention to the idea of nonrealistic setting. Students were assigned to recreate the setting of their book in a three-dimensional mode. (They had a week to complete this project.) Students gathered in their assigned groups and were asked to discuss the setting of their novels and to share their daily diaries.

Day 3: Lori conducted a minilesson on conflict, asking students to consider the internal conflict of the main character of their novel (which in every case was female). They were invited to reflect on the character's struggle to choose between who she wanted to be and who others expected or wanted her to be. The terms *expression* and *suppression* as they relate to voice were introduced, and she gave students a framework similar to that in Figure 1 (see page 23) to guide their exploration of the conflicts the main character experiences. In their groups, students completed a worksheet on conflict and continued to share their daily diaries.

Days 4 through 7: Lori reviewed plot sequence. In groups, students were asked to begin a plot diagram of their book and to continue discussing their diaries.

Day 8: By this time, students had completed most of their book, so Lori taught a minilesson on theme. She then asked students to decide in groups what they thought their novel's theme was, using the expression/suppression framework to guide their discussion.

Day 9: Lori conducted a whole-group discussion on the theme of the four books. Although it varied slightly from class to class, students agreed on the intended theme: Girls can do anything, but sometimes people or things try to stop them. The teacher asked students whether they agreed with the theme of the books, and lively discussion followed. Lori instructed students to write an essay that clearly stated the theme and gave support from the individual book they had read.

Day 10: Students revisited the prediction chart they had made on day 1 and compared their original predictions with their reading.

Student Reactions to the Books

During the first days of the unit, students read the books simply to become familiar with the setting, plot, and characters. At first, students were unclear about the terms *expression* and *suppression*, but these concepts became clearer when students were asked to consider the differences between what a character desired and what others expected of her. When students began filling in the expression/suppression framework, they had some difficulty finding examples of the various factors. For example, not many of the books focused on the heroine's appearance. Students were asked if the girls were attractive and if it mattered. Students generally agreed that beauty was helpful but not necessary. Students also recognized that in every book, girls were not able to do what they wanted to do.

By the time students examined the books' themes, they clearly understood that all focused on the roles of women in society. They were able to articulate that each author's message highlighted women's fight to achieve a place in a male society. However, reactions to this theme varied. In two of the classes, discussion about students' agreement with the theme was quite restrained; students politely stated that girls had many opportunities now and that only in the past had there been barriers to their success. Girls appeared reluctant to admit that any such barriers were still in place. Boys appeared unaware of any limitations placed on girls. At first, both boys and girls failed to see relationships between the intended theme of the books and issues in their own lives. When asked, "How does this happen now, in this school—or does it?" they were unable, or unwilling, to think of examples. It became apparent that girls were uncomfortable with the discussion. However, in two other classes, the conversation became very heated.

As we observed one of these heated discussions, we noted that girls continued to raise their hands to be called upon to speak, yet boys shouted out their comments without being given permission. Lori commented that in the most acrimonious class, the boys appeared to be entertained by the arguments, while the girls appeared to be truly angry. Lori used this episode to ask the girls, "Why do you think you are angrier than the boys?" and "Boys, why do you think the girls are so angry?" She also asked why boys were shouting out while girls were raising their hands, which helped all the students focus on the themes of expression and suppression.

To discover what students had learned from this unit, we interviewed a random selection of students, asking "What did you get out of reading your book and the class discussions?" "What do you think about the issue of women trying to get what they want?" and "Would you read more stories like this, or recommend them to your friends?" Also, we analyzed the students' final essays to identify common responses. We obtained the following generalizations:

There are societal expectations for women that are different (and often more restrictive) than those in place for men. Students recognized that the girls in the stories had to try to fit into a rules-oriented society. One student, Kody, wrote, "The princess wants to be different, and she is very tired of people trying to tell her that being different is bad and that she should try to become a regular princess." Students also recognized that today's girls have struggles as well, although there was some reluctance to admit this. In one classroom discussion, a student said, "Way back then...it was male-dominated." The fact that the fantasy genre is set "once upon a time" may have made it easier for students to dismiss female characters' struggles as anachronistic. Yet in an interview, Scott, age 12, echoed most of his classmates when he said, "I would hope and believe that girls can do what they want, but they probably wouldn't be able to...I think that we are the same."

The women in the book are strong because they are or become determined, and this is what allows them to survive. Tiffany wrote about *Ella Enchanted*, "Ella's best strength was determination. Ella never gave up. She struggled daily against her curse, even though she never won." C.J. wrote of the heroine in *Dealing with Dragons*, "One of Cimorene's strengths is that she never takes no for an answer." Both of these female characters establish a strong voice. They refuse to listen to others who urge them to passively accept their roles. These heroines demonstrate the strength that it takes to maintain a separate voice.

Sometimes women are not supportive of one another and can in fact become obstacles to one another's success. In *Dragonsinger*, as noted in Landon's paper,

> The most critical of Menolly's presence were actually the other girls in the hall. Since Menolly was receiving all the attention, the girls were

jealous. The girls decided from the very start to hold grudges against Menolly and to try to make her time at Harper Hall miserable.

To conform, girls sometimes pretend to be less capable than they are. This particular method of fitting in is used often by the protagonist of *Dragonsinger*. Lauren wrote of Menolly, "Should she play the instruments badly and make the girls happy so that they would become her friends, or should she play the instruments well and be happy with herself?"

Sometimes a girl has to run away from her home, family, or society to find her authentic voice. Candi, who read *Dealing with Dragons*, wrote, "When Cimorene ran away she changed. She became more free-willed. She was able to do things her parents thought were improper. Cimorene became stronger and more jubilant than she was before." Mike commented on the character Menolly: "She becomes very happy when she runs away. She's free to hum and sing, and she realizes she could never get herself to return." This is a message that concerns us. Running away is a dangerous idea to entertain as a solution to gender discrimination. We regret not having recognized this early enough to hold discussions on the topic and suggest that teachers address this point in classroom discussion whenever a book's plot deems it necessary.

Some of the most interesting comments we received were in response to the question, Would you read more stories like this, or recommend them to your friends? In their responses, some students clearly reflected the purpose of the study in their interviews and essays:

> Yes! It's different from most books, like, where the leading man saves women. We should see different ways. (Sam, age 12)

> Yes! Because I'm tired of happily ever after, especially since men end up the big heroes. (Charell, age 11)

Girls more often appreciated the role reversal of the main characters than boys. Occasionally, however, boys provided wonderful insights as well, which confirmed our belief that while girls reap the most benefit, both boys and girls can gain valuable perspective from reading and discussing these novels.

Summary

There are many ways to engage a whole language arts class in discussing books that highlight girls' issues. Books assigned by the school district for summer or grade-level reading often center around girls who are placed in difficult situations. These provide excellent resources for looking at the ways girls (and boys) are challenged in the society of today, the society of the past, and even ways that may evolve in the future. Teachers can use a variety of techniques to engage students in discussion. Both whole-class and literature circle structures can foster dialogue around gender and its effect on both girls and boys.

What We Hope for Our Girls

WHAT WOULD we hope to see in a school system that believes in the value of reading good literature and espouses its responsibilities toward assisting girls' development?

Walking down the halls of an elementary school during the school day, we would hear the excited voices of fifth graders as they join in a whole-class discussion of *The Witch of Blackbird Pond* (Speare, 1958/1977) as part of their study of U.S. history. They are arguing about the role of women in shaping the United States. After school hours, we stop by the library and see a group of parents and children participating in a book club. This week they are discussing *Julie of the Wolves* (George, 1974) and talking about what it would be like to be a young girl living completely on your own.

In the middle school across town, eighth-grade English classes are using literature circles in their study of fantasy novels. The teacher has chosen a mix of books, many with female protagonists. As we listen in, we hear one group of boys and girls debating whether the heroine of *Sabriel* (Nix, 1995) is a stronger character than her male counterpart, Touchstone, and why. They are puzzling over why the Abhorsen is sometimes male and sometimes female. At lunchtime, we peer into the library and see a group of girls meeting with the librarian; their book club is reading *Stargirl* (Spinelli, 2002), and they are talking about whether anyone in their school is like Stargirl. They also are wondering if they would like to be like her.

In the high school down the road, we hear an announcement about a student-teacher book club that is meeting after school that day. The book to be discussed is *Like Sisters on the Homefront* (Williams-Garcia, 1995). Two English teachers are talking in the hall about how wonderful the student-teacher book club has turned out to be, letting them get to know their students on a whole new level. One of the teachers goes on to tell about his use of discussion circles every

Friday based on young adult fiction that the students are reading. The current book, *Make Lemonade* (Wolff, 1993), has generated heated controversy about teen pregnancy and whether young mothers should keep their babies or give them up for adoption. The teacher has been able to recommend the book club as a way of furthering the discussion. A number of students are in the hall, waiting for class to start and looking over copies of *Out of the Dust* (Hesse, 1997). When we stop them and ask about the book, they explain that they are reading it in their U.S. history class as part of the study on the Great Depression. They tell us that they had no idea what it was like in the Dust Bowl of Oklahoma. They are eager to tell us about Billie Jo and how she represents the strength of women on the prairie.

Similar scenarios are occurring sporadically in schools across the United States, but nowhere have we seen a concerted effort to infuse these practices throughout the years of schooling. Yet they are very simple and economical to adopt. Using literature to focus on girls' issues is an engaging and effective way to help girls navigate the difficult ocean of adolescence. It also helps boys understand the dilemmas that girls face in trying to find their voices and relate to their female peers in a more constructive way. It helps teachers and parents appreciate what girls are experiencing, and allows them to discuss difficult questions in a safe way. As demonstrated by the scenarios we have described, it is easily inserted into the already existing structure and curricula of schools.

So what is needed to make this happen? Well-informed readers, as you are now, can look for books that open discussions about girls' issues. You can start book clubs at your schools. You can introduce parents to good books that their daughters (and sons) can read. You can recommend books to your female students, start a class library of those books, and order them for the school library. You can advocate for forums that allow girls to share their experiences, questions, and fears. In doing so, you can assist girls in finding and shaping their authentic voices. You can give them vicarious experiences that allow them to prepare for what may be dangerous—and are certainly disturbing—encounters with sex, violence, and pressure to look good.

We hope that this book has provided ideas about how you can help. Our girls are worth the effort.

REFERENCES

2006 Outward Bound Summer Expeditions. (2006). Retrieved August 10, 2006, from http://www.thompsonisland.org/english/youth/summer

Adams, D. (n.d.). *Book club corner: A brief history of book clubs.* Retrieved October 5, 2004, from http://www.co.beaufort.sc.us/bftlib/club3.htm

Adler, E., & Clark, R. (1991). Adolescence: A literary passage. *Adolescence,* *104*(26), 757–768.

Alvermann, D.E., Young, J.P., & Green, C. (1997). Adolescents' negotiations of out-of-school reading discussions. Reading Research Report No. 77. (ERIC Document Reproduction Service No. ED 403551)

American Association of University Women (AAUW) Educational Foundation. (1993). *Hostile hallways: The AAUW survey on sexual harassment in America's schools.* Washington, DC: American Association of University Women.

American Association of University Women (AAUW) Educational Foundation (1995). *How schools shortchange girls: The AAUW report.* New York: Marlowe & Company.

American Library Association. (n.d.). *The 100 most frequently challenged books of 1990–2000.* Retrieved November 4, 2004, from http://www.ala.org/ala/oif/bannedbooksweek/bbwlinks/100mostfrequently.htm

Anorexia Nervosa and Related Eating Disorders, Inc. (n.d.). *Statistics: How many people have eating disorders?* Retrieved October 13, 2004, from http://www.anred.com/stats.html

American rape statistics. (n.d.). Retrieved September 7, 2004, from http://www.par alumun.com/issuesrapestats.htm

Auerbach, N. (1978). *Communities of women: An idea in fiction.* Cambridge, MA: Harvard University Press.

Author profile: Laurie Halse Anderson. (2005). Retrieved January 30, 2004, from http://www.teenreads.com/authors/au-anderson-laurie.asp

Author profile: Shelley Fraser Mickle. (2002). Retrieved September 17, 2004, from http://www.teenreads.com/authors/au-mickle-shelley-fraser.asp

Bailey, M.D. (2002). The feminization of magic and the emerging idea of the female witch in the late middle ages. *Essays in Medieval Studies,* *19,* 120–134.

Bailey, S.M. (1996). Shortchanging girls and boys. *Educational Leadership,* *53*(8), 75–79.

Bao, W., Whitbeck, L.B., & Hoyt, D.R. (2000). Abuse, support, and depression among homeless and runaway adolescents. *Journal of Health and Social Behavior,* *41*(4), 408–420.

Barchers, S. (1988). 75 ways to share a book. *Learning,* *88,* 33.

Blume, J. (1986). *Letters to Judy: What your kids wish they could tell you.* New York: Putnam.

Body obsession starts young. (2001, July 23). *Daily Press,* n.p.

Book club. (n.d.). Retrieved on May 23, 2004, from http://chateau.neric.org/hallen/book_club.htm

Brabham, E.G., & Villaume, S.K. (2000). Questions and answers: Continuing conversations about literature circles. *The Reading Teacher, 54*(3), 278–280.

Broughton, M.A. (2002). The performance and construction of subjectivities of early adolescent girls in book club discussion groups. *Journal of Literacy Research, 34*(1), 1–38.

Brown, J. (1998). Historical fiction or fictionalized history? Problems for writers of historical novels for young adults. *ALAN Review, 26*(1), 1–7.

Brown, L.M., & Gilligan, C. (1992). *Meeting at the crossroads: Women's psychology and girls' development.* New York: Ballantine.

Brumberg, J.J. (1998). *The body project: An intimate history of American girls.* New York: Vintage.

Buist, K.L., Dekovic, M., Meeus, W., & van Aken, M.A.G. (2002). Developmental patterns in adolescent attachment to mother, father and sibling. *Journal of Youth and Adolescence, 31*(3), 167–176.

Butler, D.A., & Manning, M.L. (1998). *Addressing gender differences in young adolescents.* Olney, MD: Association for Childhood Education International.

Carico, K.M. (1996, April). *Responses of four adolescent females to adolescent fiction with strong female characters.* Paper presented at the Annual Meeting of the American Educational Research Association, New York, NY. (ERIC Document Reproduction Service No. ED 396302)

Carter, C. (1997, March). *The stuff that dreams are made of: Culture, ethnicity, class, place, and adolescent Appalachian girls' sense of self.* Paper presented at the Annual Meeting of the American Educational Research Association, Chicago, IL. (ERIC Document Reproduction Service No. ED 407 206)

Chandler, K. (1997). The beach book club: Literacy in the "lazy days of summer." *Journal of Adolescent & Adult Literacy, 41,* 104–115.

Cohen, J., & Blanc, S., (1996). *Girls in the middle: Working to succeed in school.* Washington, DC: American Association of University Women Educational Foundation.

Collins, W.A. (2003). More than myth: The developmental significance of romantic relationships during adolescence. *Journal of Research on Adolescence, 13*(1), 1–24.

Cooper-Mullin, A., & Coye, J.M. (1998). *Once upon a heroine: 400 books for girls to love.* Chicago, IL: Contemporary Books.

Crabtree, S. (2003, May). The Gallup Poll Tuesday Briefing. Retrieved December 3, 2004, from http://www.proquest.com

Croyle, W. (2003). *Children form own book club.* Retrieved May 23, 2004, from http://www.enquirer.com/editions/2003/12/08/loc_loc2book.html

Daniels, H. (2002). Resource for middle school book clubs. *Voices from the Middle, 10*(1) 48–49.

Davis, J.B., & MacGillivray, L. (2001). Books about teen parents: Messages and omissions. *English Journal, 90*(3), 90–96.

Dodson, S. (1997). *The mother-daughter book club: How ten busy mothers and daughters came together to talk, laugh and learn through their love of reading.* New York: HarperCollins.

Dodson, S. (1998). *100 books for girls to grow on.* New York: HarperCollins.

Erickson, E.H. (1993). *Childhood and society.* New York: W.W. Norton. (Original work published 1950)

Esman, A.E. (1990). *Adolescence and culture.* New York: Columbia University Press.

Fagan, P.F., & Rector, R.E. (2000). The effects of divorce on America. The Heritage Foundation Policy Research & Analysis #1373. Retrieved November 22, 2006, from http://www.dadsnow.org/studies/heritage1.htm

Farinacci, M. (1998). "We have so much to talk about": Implementing literature circles as an action-research project. *The Ohio Reading Teacher, 32*(2), 4–11.

Forum on Child and Family Statistics. (2006). America's children in brief: Key national indicators of well-being, 2006. Retrieved November 12, 2006, from http://www.childstats.gov/americaschildren/pop.asp

Geuzaine, C., Debry, M., & Liessens, V. (2000). Separation from parents in late adolescence: The same for boys and girls? *Journal of Youth and Adolescence, 29*(1), 79–91.

Gilligan, C., Lyons, N., & Hammer, T. (Eds.). (1990). *Making connections: The relational worlds of adolescent girls at Emma Willard School.* Cambridge, MA: Harvard University Press.

Go girls book club. (n.d.). Retrieved May 23, 2004, from http://bostonteachnet.org/bwm/diggs/sigproj.htm

Goodrich, N.L. (1990). *Priestesses.* New York: HarperPerennial.

Gray, H.M., & Phillips, S. (1998). *Real girl/real world: Tools for finding your true self.* Seattle, WA: Seal Press.

Haiken, M.L. (2002). Sharing "knowledge about life": Empowering adolescent girls through groups. *Voice of Youth Advocates, 24*(6), 411–415.

Hallett, M., & Karasek, B., Eds. (2002). *Folk & fairy tales.* Petersborough, ON, Canada: Broadview.

Health education standards of learning for Virginia Public schools. (April 26, 2001). Retrieved November 11, 2006, from http://www.pen.k12.va.us/VDOE/Superintendent/Sols/healthk-10.pdf

Health framework for California public schools: Kindergarten through grade twelve (2003). Retrieved November 11, 2006, from http://www.cde.ca.gov/re/pn/fd/documents/health-framework-2003.pdf

Heilman, E., & Goodman, J. (1996). Teaching gender identity in high school. *The High School Journal, 79*(3), 249–261.

Hollander, D. (2004). Changes in teenagers' sexual behavior stall. *Perspectives on Sexual and Reproductive Health, 36*(4), 141.

Hood, M.W. (1994). The delta team: Empowering adolescent girls. *Schools in the Middle, 3*(3), 24–26.

Hooper, B. (2001). The mother of all book clubs. *Booklist, 98*(2), 194–195.

Hudson, K., & Stiles, J. (1998). Single-sex classes: A plus for pre-adolescent girls. *Principal, 78*(2), 57–58.

Hupp, S. (2005, January 4). When it comes to school, girls rule. Indianapolis Star. Retrieved November 12, 2006, from http://www.overbrook.org/newsletter/girls_inc.pdf

Inglemoor High School Library Book Club (n.d.). Retrieved May 23, 2004, from http://schools.nsd.org/~tmccausland/library/BookClub.html

Irwin-DeVitis, L., & Benjamin, B. (1995). Can Anne be like Margot and still be Anne? Adolescent girls' development and *Anne Frank: The diary of a young girl. The ALAN Review, 23*(1), 10–15.

Jamison, K.R. (1999). *Night falls fast: Understanding suicide*. New York: Knopf.

Johnson, B. (2005). *How U.S. consumers spend their time*. Retrieved July 2, 2005, from http://www.adage.com/news.cms?newsId=44895.

Johnson, H. (2000). "To stand up and say something": "Girls only" literature circles at the middle level. *The New Advocate, 13*(4), 375–389.

Johnson, N.G., & Roberts, M.C. (1999). Passage on the wild river of adolescence: Arriving safely. In N.G. Johnson, M.C. Roberts, & J. Worell (Eds.), *Beyond appearance: A new look at adolescent girls* (pp. 3–18). Washington, DC: American Psychological Association.

Kaplan, A.G., Klein, R., & Gleason, N. (1991). Women's self development in late adolescence. In J.V. Jordan, A.G. Kaplan, J.B. Miller, I.P. Stiver, & J.L. Surrey (Eds.), *Women's growth in connection: Writings from the Stone Center* (pp. 122–142). New York: Guilford.

Kaplan, S.J., Labruna, V., Pelcovitz, D., Salzinger, S., Mandel, F., & Weiner, M. (1999). Physically abused adolescents: Behavior problems, functional impairment, and comparison of informants' reports [Electronic version]. *Pediatrics, 104*(1), 43–49.

Karen Hesse's interview transcript. Retrieved November 11, 2006, from http://content.scholastic.com/browse/collateral.jsp?id=1322

Kennedy, J.F. (June 11, 1963). Radio and television report to the American people on civil rights. Retrieved November 12, 2006, from http://www.jfklibrary.org/Historical+Resources/Archives/Reference+Desk/Speeches/JFK/003POF03CivilRights06111963.htm

King, M.L. (August 28, 1963). I have a dream. Retrieved November 14, 2006, from http://www.americanrhetoric.com/speeches/mlkihaveadream.htm

Kirby, D. (2001). *Emerging answers: Research findings on programs to reduce teen pregnancy (summary)* [Electronic version]. Retrieved November 15, 2006, from http://www.teenpregnancy.org/resources/data/pdf/emeranswsum.pdf

Koplewicz, H.S. (2002). *More than moody: Recognizing and treating adolescent depression*. New York: Putnam.

Larson, R., Wilson, S., Brown, B.B., Furstenberg, F.F., Jr, & Verma, S. (2002). Changes in adolescents' interpersonal experiences: Are they being prepared for adult relationships in the 21st century? *Journal of Research on Adolescence, 12*(1), 31–68.

Laskin, D., & Hughes, H. (1995). *The reading group book: The complete guide to starting and sustaining a reading group, with annotated lists of 250 titles for provocative discussion*. New York: Plume/Putnam.

Lieberman, R. (2004). Understanding and responding to students who self-mutilate. *Principal Leadership, 4*(7), 10–13.

Long, E. (2003). *Book clubs: Women and the uses of reading in everyday life*. Chicago : University of Chicago Press.

Lucas, K. (1999, April). *Mentoring in adolescence: A sociocultural and developmental study of undergraduate women and sixth-grade girls paired in a mentoring program*. Paper presented at the Annual Meeting of the American Educational Research Association, Montreal, Quebec, Canada. (ERIC Document Reproduction Service No. ED 429 985).

MacDorman, M.F., Minino, A.M., Strobino, D.M., & Guyer, B. (2001). Annual summary of vital statistics—2001. *Pediatrics, 110*(6), 1037–1052.

MacLeod, A.S. (1998). Writing backward: Modern models in historical fiction. *Horn Book Magazine.* Retrieved August 27, 2005, from http://www.hbook.com/exhibit/article_macleod.html

MacRae, C.D. (1998). *Presenting young adult fantasy fiction.* New York: Twayne.

Mayor Daley's elementary book club. (2003). Retrieved July 8, 2004, from http://mdbc.cps.k12.il.us/about.html

McCracken, N.M. (1992). Re-gendering the reading of literature. In N.M. McCracken & B.C. Appleby (Eds.), *Gender issues in the teaching of English* (pp. 55–68). Portsmouth, NH: Boynton/Cook.

McHale, S.M., Crouter, A.C., & Whiteman, S.D. (2003). The family contexts of gender development in childhood and adolescence. *Social Development, 12*(1), 125–148.

McMahon, S.I., & Raphael, T.E., (Eds.). (1997). *The book club connection: Literacy learning and classroom talk.* New York: Teachers College Press.

Michel, A. (1986). *Down with stereotypes: Eliminating sexism from children's literature and school textbooks.* Paris: UNESCO.

Muehlenkamp, J.L., & Gutierrez, P.M. (2004). An investigation of differences between self-injurious behavior and suicide attempts in a sample of adolescents. *Suicide and Life-Threatening Behavior, 34*(1), 12–23.

Muten, B. (2003). *Goddesses: A world of myth and magic.* Cambridge, MA: Barefoot Books.

National Council of Teachers of English. (1990a). *Guidelines for a gender-balanced curriculum in English grades 7–12.* Retrieved March 1, 2006, from http://www.ncte.org/about/over/positions/category/lit/116049.htm?source=gs.

National Council of Teachers of English. (1990b). *Guidelines for a gender-balanced curriculum in English grades PreK–6.* Retrieved March 1, 2006, from http://www.ncte.org/about/over/positions/category/lit/107636.htm.

Nilsen, A.P., & Donelson, K.L. (2001). *Literature for today's young adults* (6th ed.). New York: Addison-Wesley Longman.

Nilsen, A.P., & Donelson, K.L. (2005). *Literature for today's young adults* (7th ed.). New York: Addison-Wesley Longman.

Nodelman, P., & Reimer, M. (2003). *The pleasures of children's literature.* Boston, MA: Pearson.

Noring, S. (2000). Child abuse and neglect: A look at the states [Electronic version]. *American Journal of Public Health, 90*(4), 635.

Odean, K. (1997). *Great books for girls.* New York: Ballantine.

Orenstein, P. (1994). *Schoolgirls: Young women, self-esteem, and the confidence gap.* New York: Anchor Books, Doubleday.

Peck, R. (Winter, 1978). Rape and the teenage victim. *Top of the News,* 173–177.

Pierce, T. (1993). Fantasy: Why kids read it, why kids need it. *School Library Journal, 39,* 50–51.

Pipher, M. (1994). *Reviving Ophelia: Saving the selves of adolescent girls.* New York: Ballantine.

Porter, T. (1996). Connecting with Courage: An Outward Bound program for adolescent girls. *Women's Voices in Experiential Education.* (ERIC Document Reproduction Service No. ED 412 051)

Rape, Abuse, & Incest National Network. (2006). *Statistics*. Retrieved April 28, 2006, from http://www.rainn.org/statistics

Raphael, T.E., Kehus, M., & Damphousse, K. (2001). *Book club for middle school*. Lawrence, MA: Small Planet Communications.

ReadWriteThink. (n.d.). *Book clubs: Reading for fun*. Retrieved May 13, 2004, from http://www.readwritethink.org/lessons/lesson_view.asp?id=67

Rodney, E.B., & Young, R. (Producers). (1954–1963). *Father knows best* [Television series]. Los Angeles: CBS Broadcasting.

Rothenberg, D. (1997). *Supporting girls in early adolescence*. (ERIC Document Reproduction Service No. ED 408 031). Retrieved November 22, 2006, from http://www.ericdigests.org/1996-2/girls.html

Rubin, R. (2001, April 18). Teen birth rates drop to a new low. *USA Today*, n.p.

Saal, R. (1995). *The New York Public Library guide to reading groups*. New York: Crown.

Sadker, M., & Sadker, D.M. (1994). *Failing at fairness: How our schools cheat girls*. New York: Touchstone.

Safire, W. (2000, August 27). Lookism. *New York Times Magazine*. Retrieved March 1, 2006, from http://partners.nytimes.com/library/magazine/home/20000827mag-onlanguage.html

Shandler, S. (1999). *Ophelia speaks: Adolescent girls write about their search for self*. New York: HarperPerennial.

Smith, S.A. (1997, March). *Book club is "da bomb": Early adolescent girls engage with texts, transactions, and talk*. Paper presented at the Annual Meeting of the American Educational Research Association, Chicago, IL. (ERIC Document Reproduction Service No ED 407650)

Smith, S. (2001, April). *"What we are and what we're not": Early adolescent girls negotiate their identities through talk about text*. Paper presented at the Annual Meeting of the American Educational Research Association, Seattle, WA. (ERIC Document Reproduction Service No ED 452483)

Sprague, M.M. (2003). An academy for Ophelia? *Clearing House*, 76(4), 178–184.

Sprague, M.M., & Keeling, K.K. (2000). A library for Ophelia. *Journal of Adolescent & Adult Literacy*, 43, 640–647.

Sprague, M.M., & Risher, L. (2002). Using fantasy literature to explore gender issues. *ALAN Review*, 29(2), 39–42.

Stone, K. (2002). The misuses of enchantment. In M. Hallett, & B. Karasek (Eds.), *Folk & fairy tales* (pp. 391–414). Petersborough, ON, Canada: Broadview.

Stover, L.S. (1992). Re-gendering the reading of literature. In N.M. McCracken & B.C. Appleby (Eds.), Gender issues in the teaching of English, (pp. 93–110). Portsmouth, NH: Boynton/Cook.

Striegel-Moore, R., & Cachelin, F.M. (1999). Body image concerns and disordered eating in adolescent girls: Risk and protective factors. In N.G. Johnson, M.C. Roberts, & J. Worell (Eds.), *Beyond appearance: A new look at adolescent girls* (pp. 85–108). Washington, DC: American Psychological Association.

Thomas, J.J., & Daubman, K.A. (2001). The relationship between friendship quality and self-esteem in adolescent girls and boys. *Sex Roles*, 45(1/2), 53–65.

Thomas, K. (2002, February 27). Girls are drinking like boys: Teen's alcohol use now nearly equal. *USA Today*, n.p.

Trimel, S. (2000). Grace Christ examines how children deal with grief. *Columbia News*. Retrieved November 29, 2004, from http://www.columbia.edu/cu/news/00/02/graceChrist.html

Trites, R.S. (1997). *Waking Sleeping Beauty: Feminist voices in children's novels*. Iowa City: University of Iowa Press.

Trites, R.S. (2000). *Disturbing the universe: Power and repression in adolescent literature*. Iowa City: University of Iowa Press.

U.S. Department of Labor. (n.d.) Title IX, Education Amendments of 1972. Retrieved November 11, 2006, from http://www.dol.gov/oasam/regs/statutes/titleix.htm

Viadero, D. (2006). Concern over gender gaps shifting to boys. *Education Week*, *25*(7), 1–3.

Vignoles, V., Regalia, C., Manzi, C., Golledge, J., & Scabini, E. (2006). Beyond self-esteem: Influence of multiple motives on identity construction. *Journal of Personality and Social Psychology*, *90*(2), 308–333.

Warner, M. (2002). Go! Be a beast: Beauty and the beast. In M. Hallett & B. Karasek (Eds.), *Folk & fairy tales* (pp. 415–427). Petersborough, ON, Canada: Broadview.

Whaley, L., & Dodge, L. (1999). *Weaving in the women: Transforming the high school English curriculum*. Portsmouth, NH: Boynton/Cook.

Women's Educational Media. (n.d.) That's a family! Statistics on US Families. Retrieved November 12, 2006, from http://www.womedia.org/taf_statistics.htm

CHAPTER 1

Anderson, L.H. (2003). *Speak*. New York: Penguin Putnam.

Cleary, B. (2003). *Fifteen*. New York: HarperTrophy. (Original work published 1956)

CHAPTER 2

Alcott, L.M. (1947). *Little women*. New York: Grossett & Dunlop. (Original work published 1867)

Allende, I. (Ed). (2000). *These are not sweet girls: Poetry by Latin American women* (Secret Weavers series). Buffalo, NY: White Pine Press. (Original work published 1994)

Anderson, L.H. (2003). *Speak*. New York: Penguin Putnam.

Avi. (1992). *The true confessions of Charlotte Doyle*. New York: Avon Books.

Baczewski, P. (1990). *Just for kicks*. Baltimore: Lippincott, Williams & Wilkins.

Blume, J. (1972). *Are you there, God? It's me, Margaret*. New York: Dell Yearling.

Bruckheimer, J. (Producer) & Scott, R. (Director). (2001). *Black hawk down* [Motion picture]. United States: Sony.

Creech, S. (2000). *The wanderer*. New York: Joanna Cotler Books.

Crutcher, C. (2003). *Staying fat for Sarah Byrnes*. New York: HarperTempest. (Original work published 1993)

Cushman, K. (1995). *Catherine, called Birdy*. New York: HarperTrophy.

Duffy, C.A. (Ed.). (1997). *I wouldn't thank you for a valentine: Poems for young feminists*. New York: Henry Holt.

Goldwyn, S. (Producer) & Weir, P. (Writer/Director). (2003). *Master and commander: The far side of the world* [Motion picture]. United States: Twentieth Century Fox.

Haddix, M.P. (2001). *Just Ella*. New York: Aladdin Paperbacks.

Konigsburg, E.L. (1998). *From the mixed-up files of Mrs. Basil E. Frankweiler*. New York: Aladdin. (Original work published 1967)

L'Engle, M. (1981). *A ring of endless light*. New York: Dell Laurel-Leaf.

Levine, G.C. (1998). *Ella enchanted*. New York: HarperTrophy.

Levy, M. (1996). *Run for your life*. New York: Putnam Juvenile.

McCaffrey, A. (1997). *Dragonsinger* (Harper Hall Trilogy, Volume 2). New York: Spectra/Bantam Dell. (Original work published 1977)

McCaffrey, A. (2003). *Dragonsong* (Harper Hall Trilogy, Volume 1). New York: Aladdin Paperbacks. (Original work published 1976)

Misiroglu, G.R. (Ed.). (1999). *Girls like us: 40 extraordinary women celebrate girlhood in story, poetry, and song*. Novato, CA: New World Library.

Paterson, K. (1991). *Lyddie*. New York: Penguin Books.

Pullman, P. (2001). *The golden compass*. (His Dark Materials series, Book I). New York: Dell Yearling.

Rowling, J.K. (1998). *Harry Potter and the sorcerer's stone*. New York: Scholastic.

Segan, A.L. (Producer) & Spielberg, S. (Director). (1998). *Saving Private Ryan* [Motion picture]. United States: Dreamworks.

Spinelli, J. (1993). *There's a girl in my hammerlock*. New York: Simon & Schuster.

Tate, E.E. (1987). *The secret of Gumbo Grove*. New York: Dell Yearling.

Voigt, C. (1986). *Come a stranger*. New York: Aladdin Paperbacks.

Voigt, C. (1995). *Izzy, willy-nilly*. New York: Aladdin Paperbacks.

Walter, M.P. (1985). *Trouble's child*. New York: Lothrop, Lee & Shepard.

Wrede, P.C. (1990). *Dealing with dragons*. New York: Scholastic.

CHAPTER 3

Anderson, L.H. (2003). *Speak*. New York: Penguin Putnam.

Anonymous. (1998). *Go ask Alice*. New York: Simon Pulse. (Original work published 1967)

Blume, J. (1975). *Forever*. New York: Pocket Books.

Burgess, M. (1999). *Smack*. New York: AvonTempest.

Creech, S. (1996). *Walk two moons*. New York: HarperTrophy.

Crutcher, C. (1989). *Chinese handcuffs*. New York: Greenwillow Press.

Crutcher, C. (2003). *Staying fat for Sarah Byrnes*. New York: HarperTempest.

Hinton, S.E. (2003). *The outsiders*. New York: Speak. (Original work published 1967)

Johnson, A. (2003). *The first part last*. New York: Simon & Schuster.

Levenkron, S. (1998). *The luckiest girl in the world*. New York: Penguin.

Levy, M. (1996). *Run for your life*. New York: Putnam Juvenile.

Mackler, C. (2003). *The earth, my butt, and other round things*. Cambridge, MA: Candlewick Press.

McCormick, P. (2000). *Cut*. New York: Scholastic.

Mickle, S.F. (2001). *The turning hour*. Montgomery, AL: River City.

Naylor, P.R. (2001). *Alice on the outside*. New York: Simon Pulse.

Newman, L. (1996). *Fat chance*. New York: PaperStar.

Peck, R. (1976). *Are you in the house alone?* New York: Puffin.

Pelzer, D. (1993). *A child called "It": One child's courage to survive*. Omaha, NE: Omaha Press.

Sones, S. (2004). *One of those hideous books where the mother dies*. New York: Simon & Schuster.

Spinelli, J. (2002). *Stargirl*. New York: Knopf.

Voigt, C. (1995). *Izzy, willy-nilly*. New York: Aladdin Paperbacks.

Voigt, C. (2002). *Homecoming*. (Tillerman saga, Volume one). New York: Simon Pulse.

Williams-Garcia, R. (1995). *Like sisters on the homefront*. New York: Puffin.

Wittlinger, E. (2001). *Hard love*. New York: Simon Pulse.

Wolff, V.E. (1993). *Make lemonade*. New York: Scholastic.

CHAPTER 4

Anderson, L.H. (2002). *Fever: 1793*. New York: Aladdin Paperbacks.

Avi. (1992). *The true confessions of Charlotte Doyle*. New York: Avon Books.

Cushman, K. (1995). *Catherine, called Birdy*. New York: HarperTrophy.

Donnelly, J. (2003). *A northern light*. New York: Harcourt Paperbacks.

Dreiser, T. (2000). An American tragedy. NY: New American Library, Signet Classic. (Original work published 1925)

Hesse, K. (1997). *Out of the dust*. New York: Scholastic Signature.

O'Dell, S. (1960). *Island of the blue dolphins*. New York: Houghton Mifflin.

Paterson, K. (1991). *Lyddie*. New York: Penguin Books.

Speare, E. (1977). *The witch of Blackbird Pond*. Boston: Dell. (Original work published 1958)

CHAPTER 5

Andersen, H.C. (2002). The little mermaid. In Hallett, M. & Karasek, B., (Eds.), *Folk & fairy tales* (pp. 217–237). Petersborough, ON, Canada: Broadview. (Original story published 1836)

Baum, L.F. (1993). *The wizard of Oz*. New York: Tor Classics. (Original work published 1900)

Carroll, G., Giler, D., & Hill, W. (Producers) & Scott, R. (Director). (1979). *Alien* [Motion picture]. United States: Twentieth Century Fox.

Daly, J., Gibson, D., & Hurd, G.A. (Producers) & Cameron, J. (Director). (1984). *The Terminator* [Motion picture]. United States: Universal Studios.

Ewing, L. (2000a). *Goddess of the night* (Daughters of the Moon series, Book 1). New York: Hyperion.

Ewing, L. (2000b). *Into the cold fire* (Daughters of the Moon series, Book 2). New York: Hyperion.

Ewing, L. (2001a). *Night shade* (Daughters of the Moon series, Book 3). New York: Volo.

Ewing, L. (2001b). *Secret scroll* (Daughters of the Moon series, Book 4). New York: Volo.

Fletcher, S. (1992). *Dragon's milk* (The Dragon Chronicles, Book I). New York: Aladdin Paperbacks.

Fletcher, S. (1999). *Sign of the dove* (The Dragon Chronicles, Book III). New York: Aladdin Paperbacks.

Grimm, J.L.K., & Grimm, W.K. (1977). *Grimm's tales for young and old*. New York: Doubleday & Company. (Original work published 1819)

Haddix, M.P. (2001). *Just Ella*. New York: Aladdin Paperbacks.

Harrison, L. (2004a). *The clique*. New York: Little, Brown Young Readers.

Harrison, L. (2004b). *Best friends for never* (The clique, no. 2). New York: Little, Brown Young Readers.

Harrison, L. (2005a). *The revenge of the wannabees* (The clique, no.3). New York: Little, Brown Young Readers.

Harrison, L. (2005b). *Invasion of the body snatcher* (The clique, no. 4). New York: Little, Brown Young Readers.

Harrison, L. (2006a). *The pretty committee strikes back* (The clique, no. 5). New York: Little, Brown Young Readers.

Harrison, L. (2006b). *Dial L for loser* (The clique, no. 6). New York: Little, Brown Young Readers.

Hughes, M. (2000). *Keeper of the Isis light*. New York: Aladdin Paperbacks.

Jackson, P. (Director/producer). (2001). *Lord of the rings: Fellowship of the ring* [Motion picture]. Los Angeles: New Line Cinema.

Jackson, P. (Director/producer). (2002). *Lord of the rings: The two towers* [Motion picture]. Los Angeles: New Line Cinema.

Jackson, P. (Director/producer). (2003). *Lord of the rings: Return of the king* [Motion picture]. Los Angeles: New Line Cinema.

Klause, A.C. (1997). *Blood and chocolate.* New York: Delacorte.

L'Engle, M. (1962). *A wrinkle in time.* New York: Dell.

Lucas, G. (Director/producer). (1999). *The phantom menace* [Motion picture]. Los Angeles: 20th Century Fox.

Lucas, G. (Director/producer). (2002). *Attack of the clones* [Motion picture]. Los Angeles: 20th Century Fox.

Lucas, G. (Director/producer). (2005). *Revenge of the Sith* [Motion picture]. Los Angeles: 20th Century Fox.

Levine, G.C. (1998). *Ella enchanted.* New York: HarperTrophy.

Marillier, J. (2000). *Daughter of the forest.* New York: Tor.

McCaffrey, A. (1997). *Dragonsinger* (Harper Hall Trilogy, Volume 2). New York: Spectra/Bantam Dell. (Original work published 1977)

McCaffrey, A. (2003). *Dragonsong* (Harper Hall Trilogy, Volume 1). New York: Aladdin Paperbacks. (Original work published 1976)

McKinley, R. (1978). *Beauty: A retelling of the story of Beauty and the Beast.* New York: Harper & Row.

McKinley, R. (1982). *The blue sword.* New York: Greenwillow.

McKinley, R. (2000). *Spindle's end.* New York: Putnam.

Musker, J. (Producer) & Clements, E. (Director/Writer). (1989). *The little mermaid* [Motion picture]. United States: Walt Disney Pictures.

Nix, G. (1995). *Sabriel.* New York: Harper Collins.

Nix, G. (2001). *Lirael, daughter of the Clayr.* New York: HarperCollins.

Nix, G. (2004). *Abhorsen.* New York: Eos.

Pierce, T. (1983). *Alanna: The first adventure* (Song of the lioness series, Book 1). New York: Random House.

Pierce, T. (1990). *In the hands of the goddess* (Song of the lioness series, Book 2). New York: Random House.

Pierce, T. (2002). *The woman who rides like a man* (Song of the lioness series, Book 3). New York: Random House.

Pullman, P. (2001). *The golden compass* (His Dark Materials series, Book I). New York: Dell Yearling.

Pullman, P. (2003a). *The subtle knife* (His Dark Materials series, Book II). New York: Laurel Leaf.

Pullman, P. (2003b). *The amber spyglass* (His Dark Materials series, Book III). New York: Yearling.

Shakespeare, W. (2004). *Macbeth* (Folger Shakespeare Library). New York: Washington Square Press. (Original work published 1623)

Shelley, M. (2004). *Frankenstein.* New York: Pocket Books. (Original work published 1818)

Velde, V.V. (1995). *Companions of the night.* New York: Harcourt.

Wrede, P. (1990). *Dealing with dragons* (Book I of the The Enchanted Forest Chronicles). New York: Scholastic.

Wrede, P. (1991). *Searching for dragons* (Book 2 of the The Enchanted Forest Chronicles). New York: Jane Yolen Books.

Wrede, P. (2003a). *Calling on dragons* (Book 3 of the The Enchanted Forest Chronicles). New York: Magic Carpet Books

Wrede, P. (2003b). *Talking to dragons* (Book 4 of the The Enchanted Forest Chronicles). New York: Magic Carpet Books

Yolen, J. (2003a). *Sister light, sister dark* (Book 1 of the Great Alta Saga). New York: Tor.

Yolen, J. (2003b). *White Jenna* (Book 2 of the Great Alta Saga). New York: Tor.

CHAPTER 6

Avi. (1992). *The true confessions of Charlotte Doyle*. New York: Avon Books.

Block, F.L. (2000). *I was a teenage fairy*. New York: HarperCollins.

DiNovi, D., Swicord, R., & Carr, W. (Producers) & Armstrong, G. & Lewis, M. (Directors). (1994). *Little women* [Motion picture]. United States: Sony.

Frank, A. (1953). *Anne Frank: The diary of a young girl*. New York: Pocket Books.

Guy, R. (1992). *The friends*. New York: Dell Laurel-Leaf. (Original work published 1973)

Hesse, K. (1995). *Phoenix rising*. New York: Puffin.

Lee, H. (1988). *To kill a mockingbird*. New York: Warner. (Original work published 1960)

Levine, G.C. (1998). *Ella enchanted*. New York: HarperTrophy.

Nelson, T. (1994). *The beggar's ride*. New York: Dell. (Original work published 1992)

Nye, N.S. (1999). *Habibi*. New York: Simon Pulse.

Paterson, K. (1991). *Lyddie*. New York: Penguin.

Staples, S.F. (2000). *Shabanu: Daughter of the wind*. New York: Dell Laurel-Leaf.

Taylor, M.D. (1991). *Roll of thunder, hear my cry*. New York: Puffin. (Original work published 1976)

Woodson, J. (1995). *I hadn't meant to tell you this*. New York: Dell Laurel-Leaf.

CHAPTER 7

Anderson, L.H. (2002). *Fever: 1793*. New York: Aladdin.

Anderson, L.H. (2003). *Speak*. New York: Penguin Putnam.

Angelou, M. (1983). *I know why the caged bird sings*. New York: Bantam. (Original work published 1970)

Curtis, C.P. (1995). *The Watsons go to Birmingham—1963*. New York: Bantam Doubleday.

Houston, J., & Houston, J.D. (1983). *Farewell to Manzanar: A true story of Japanese American experience during and after the World War II internment*. New York: Dell Laurel-Leaf.

Lee, H. (1988). *To kill a mockingbird*. New York: Warner. (Original work published 1960)

Levine, G.C. (1998). *Ella enchanted*. New York: HarperTrophy.

McCaffrey, A. (1997). *Dragonsinger* (Harper Hall Trilogy, Volume 2). New York: Spectra/Bantam Dell. (Original work published 1977)

McCaffrey, A. (2003). *Dragonsong* (Harper Hall Trilogy, Volume 1). New York: Aladdin Paperbacks. (Original work published 1976)

Parks, R. (1999). *Rosa Parks: My story*. New York: Puffin. (Original work published 1990)

Porter, C. (2000). *Imani, all mine*. New York: Mariner.

Taylor, M.D. (1975). *Song of the trees*. New York: Dial.

Taylor, M.D. (1991). *Roll of thunder, hear my cry*. New York: Puffin. (Original work published 1976)

Van Draanen, W. (2001). *Flipped*. New York: Knopf.

Wrede, P. (1990). *Dealing with dragons*. New York: Scholastic.

EPILOGUE

George, J.C. (1974). *Julie of the wolves*. New York: HarperTrophy.

Hesse, K. (1997). *Out of the dust*. New York: Scholastic Signature.

Nix, G. (1995). *Sabriel*. New York: HarperCollins.

Speare, E. (1977). *The witch of Blackbird Pond*. Boston: Dell. (Original work published 1958)

Spinelli, J. (2002). *Stargirl*. New York: Knopf Books for Young Readers.

Williams-Garcia, R. (1995). *Like sisters on the homefront*. New York: Puffin.

Wolff, V.E. (1993). *Make lemonade*. New York: Scholastic.

Note: Page numbers followed by *f* indicate figures.

Note: Page numbers followed by *f* indicate figures.